EASY GUITAR
WITH NOTES & TAB

SOUTHERN ROCK HITS

ISBN 978-1-4234-9608-3

HAL•LEONARD®
CORPORATION
7777 W. BLUEMOUND RD. P.O. BOX 13819 MILWAUKEE, WI 53213

STRUM AND PICK PATTERNS

This chart contains the suggested strum and pick patterns that are referred to by number at the beginning of each song in this book. The symbols ⊓ and ∨ in the strum patterns refer to down and up strokes, respectively. The letters in the pick patterns indicate which right-hand fingers play which strings.

p = thumb
i = index finger
m = middle finger
a = ring finger

For example; Pick Pattern 2
is played: thumb - index - middle - ring

Strum Patterns   ## Pick Patterns

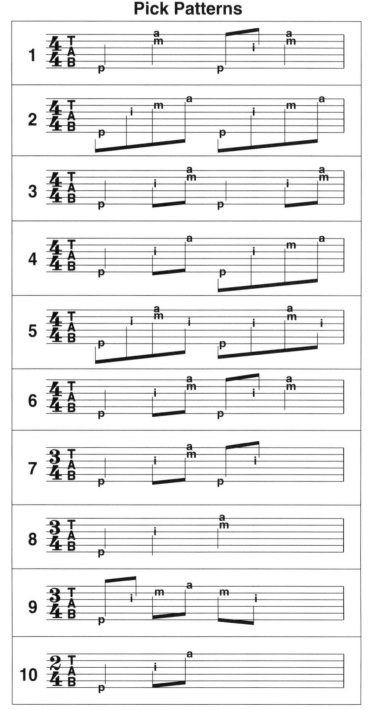

Can't You See

Words and Music by Toy Caldwell

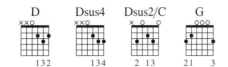

Strum Pattern: 2
Pick Pattern: 4

Intro
Moderately, in 2

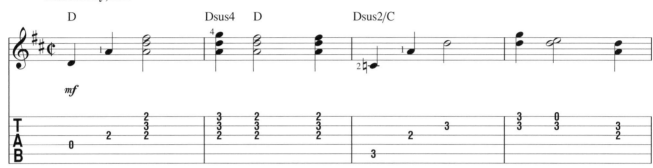

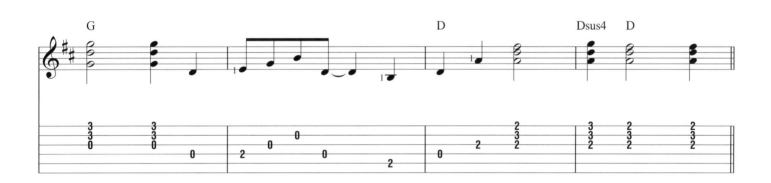

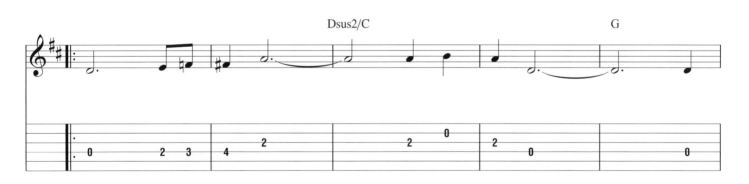

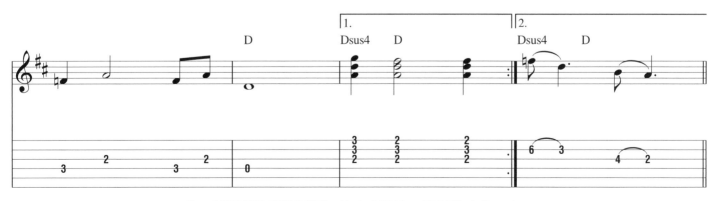

Guitar Solo

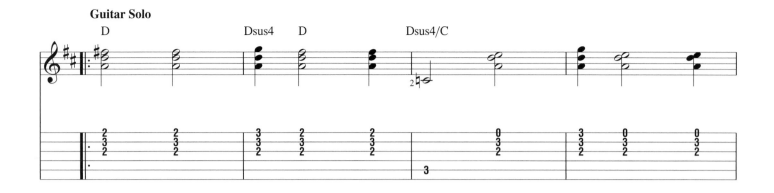

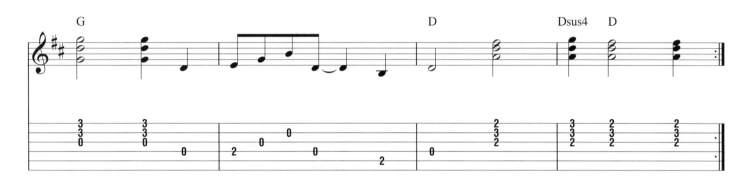

𝄋 **Verse**

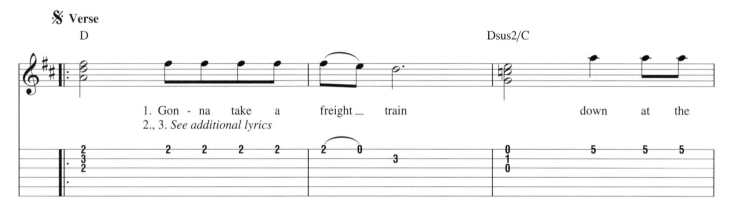

1. Gon - na take a freight train down at the
2., 3. *See additional lyrics*

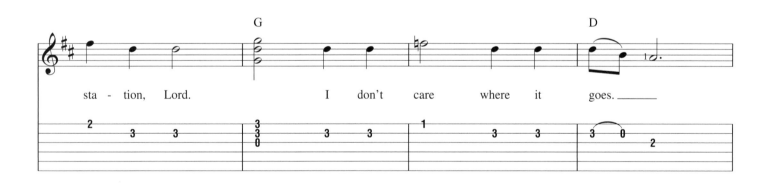

sta - tion, Lord. I don't care where it goes.

Gon - na climb a moun - tain, the high - est

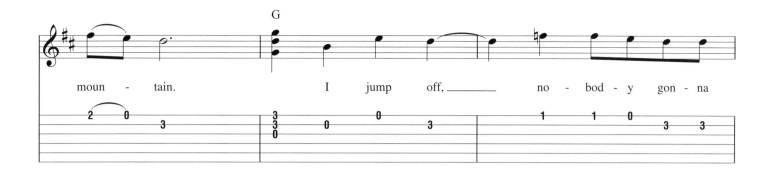

mountain.   I   jump   off, _____   no - bod - y   gon - na

Chorus

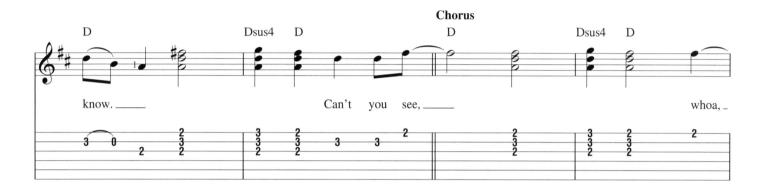

know. _____   Can't   you   see, _____   whoa, _

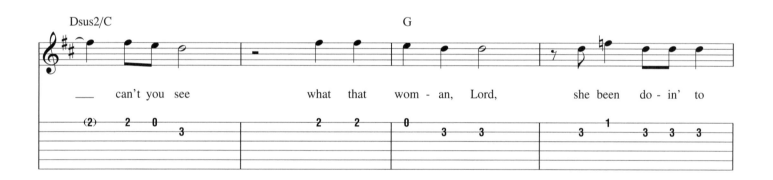

_ can't you see   what that   wom - an, Lord,   she been do - in' to

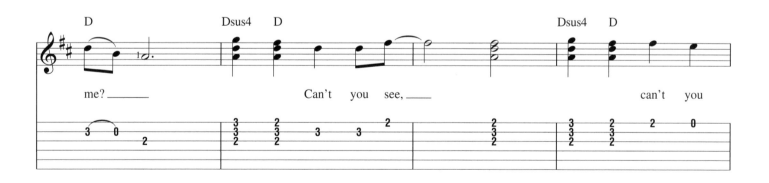

me? _____   Can't   you   see, _____   can't   you

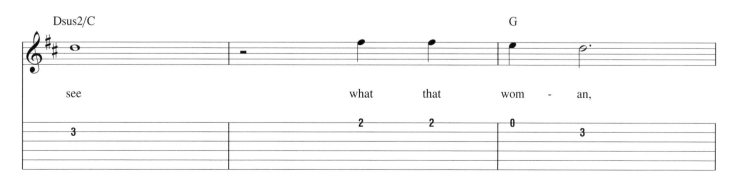

see   what that   wom - an,

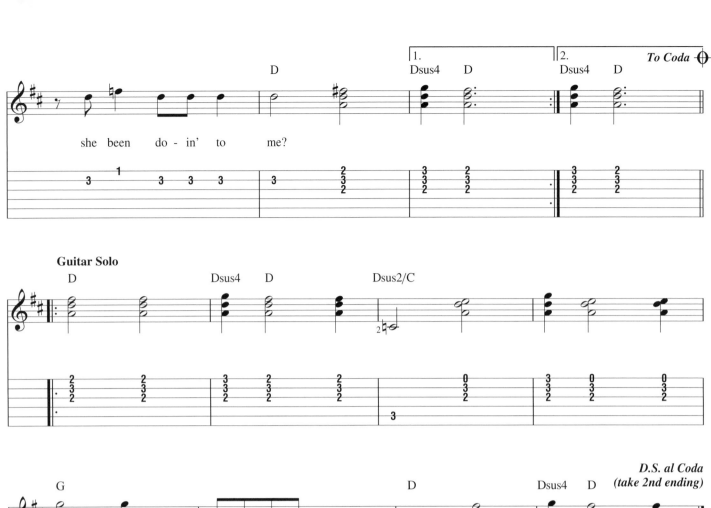

she been do - in' to me?

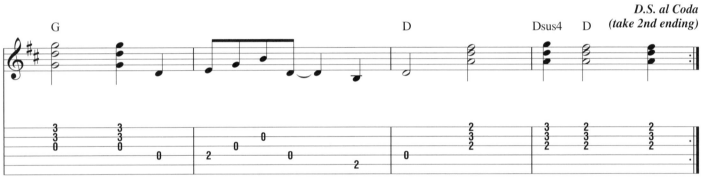

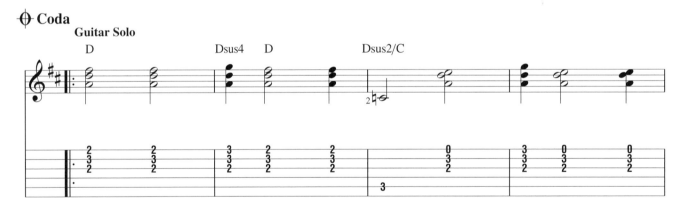

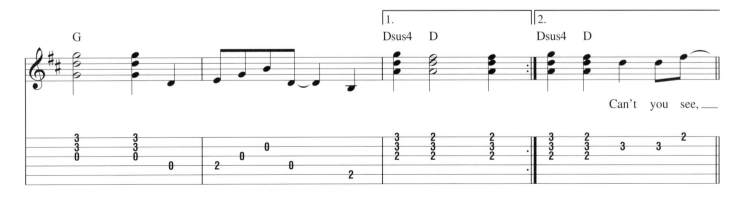

Can't you see, ___

Chorus

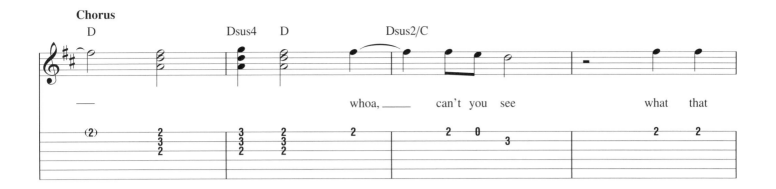

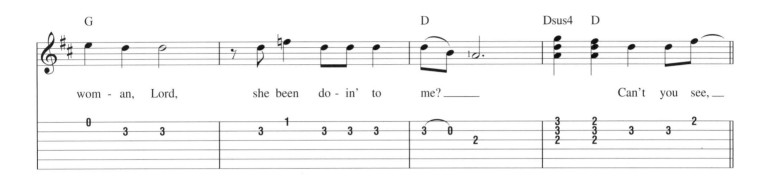

Outro

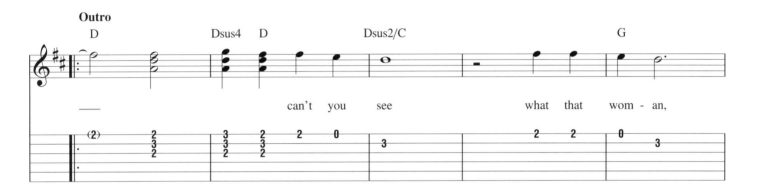

Repeat and fade

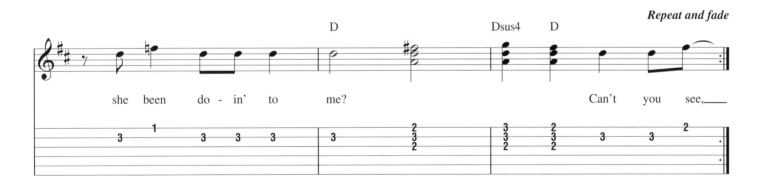

Additional Lyrics

2. I'm gonna find me a hole in the wall.
   Im gonna crawl inside and die.
   'Cause my lady now, a mean old woman, Lord,
   Never told me goodbye.

3. I'm gonna buy a ticket, now, as far as I can.
   Ain't never comin' back.
   Grab me a south bound all the way to Georgia now,
   Till the train, it run out of track.

Black Betty

New words and new music adaptation by Huddie Ledbetter

*Optional: To match recording, place capo at 2nd fret.

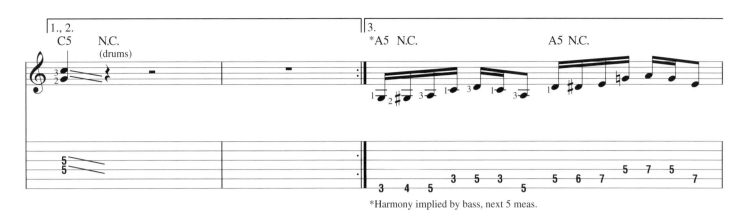

*Harmony implied by bass, next 5 meas.

Strum Pattern: 5
Pick Pattern: 4

Guitar Solo

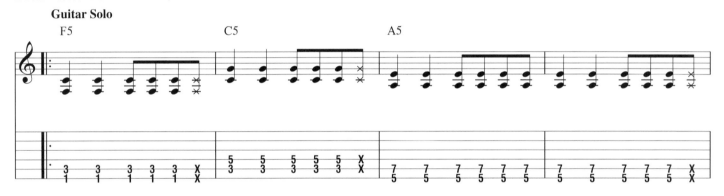

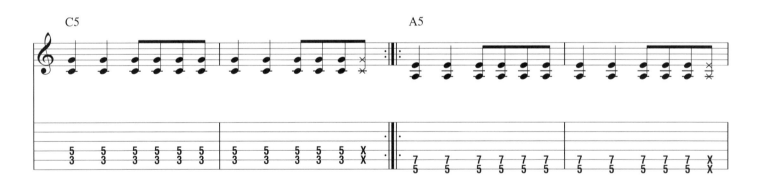

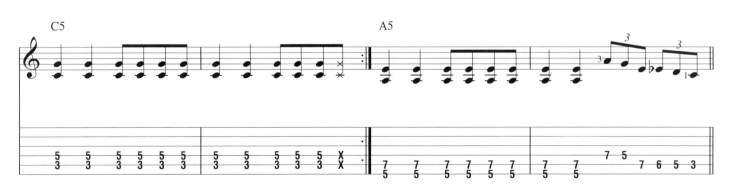

The Devil Went Down to Georgia

**Words and Music by Charlie Daniels, John Thomas Crain, Jr., William Joel DiGregorio,
Fred Laroy Edwards, Charles Fred Hayward and James Wainwright Marshall**

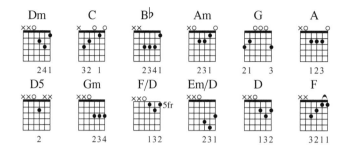

Strum Pattern: 3, 4
Pick Pattern: 4, 5

Intro
Fast Country

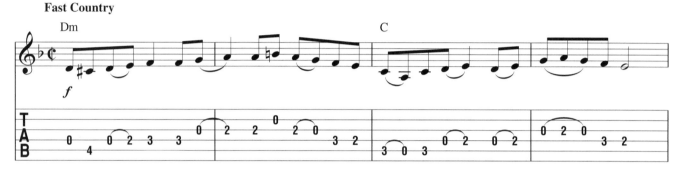

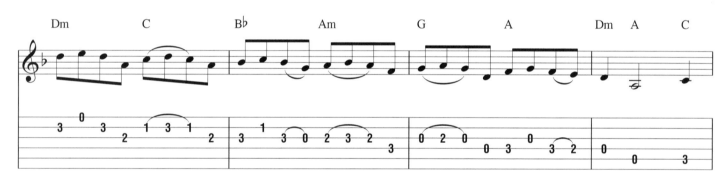

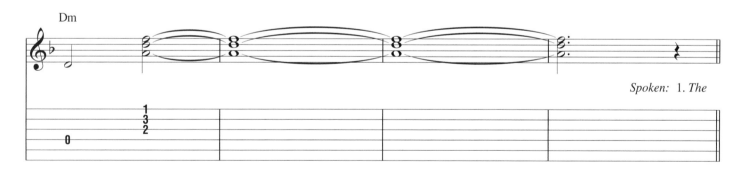

Spoken: 1. *The*

Verse

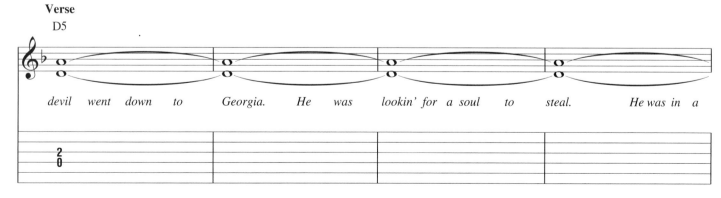

devil went down to Georgia. He was lookin' for a soul to steal. He was in a

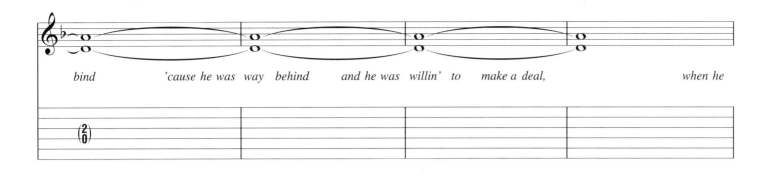

bind   'cause he was way behind   and he was willin' to   make a deal,   when he

N.C.

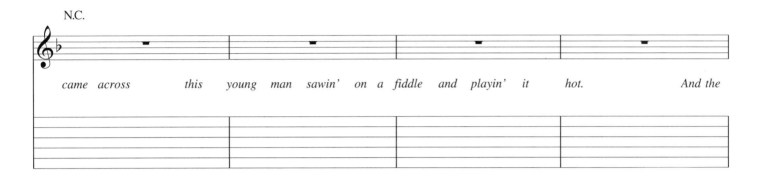

came across   this   young man sawin' on a fiddle and playin' it   hot.   And the

A   C

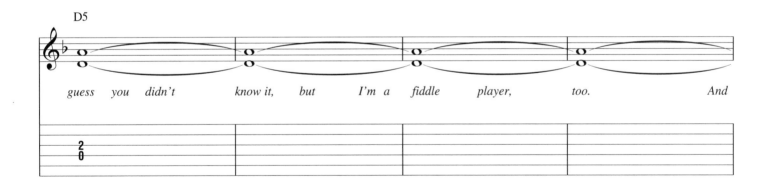

devil jumped up   on a hickory   stump and said, "Boy,   let me tell you what.   I

D5

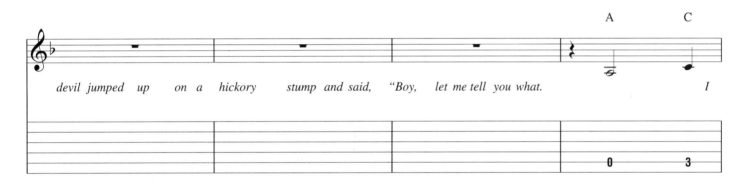

guess you didn't   know it, but I'm a fiddle   player,   too.   And

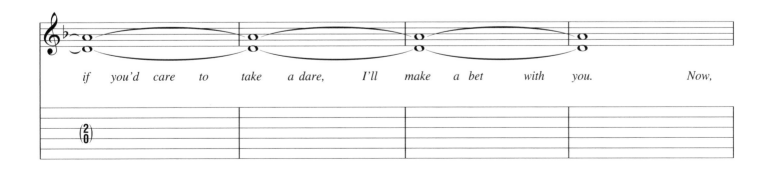

if you'd care to take a dare,   I'll make a bet   with   you.   Now,

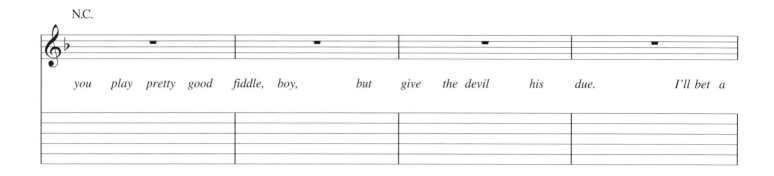

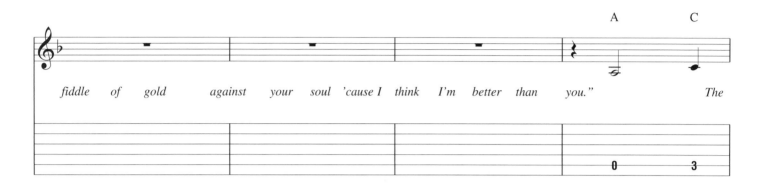

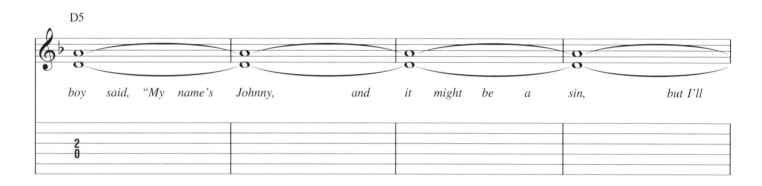

Chorus

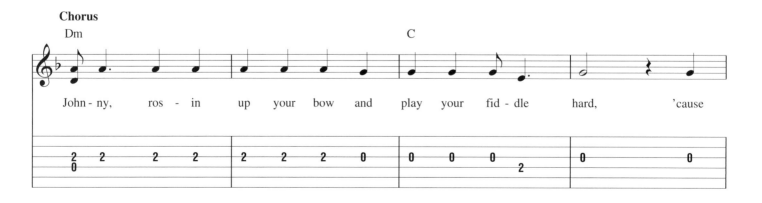

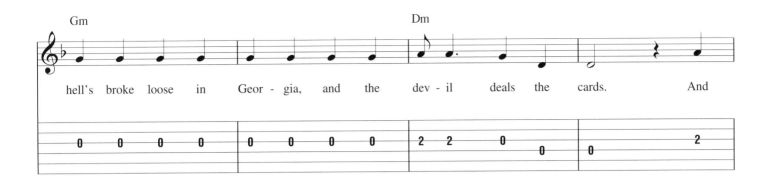

hell's broke loose in Geor - gia, and the dev - il deals the cards. And

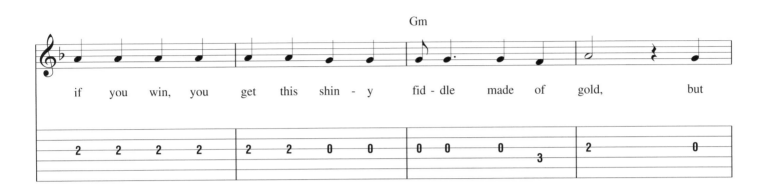

if you win, you get this shin - y fid - dle made of gold, but

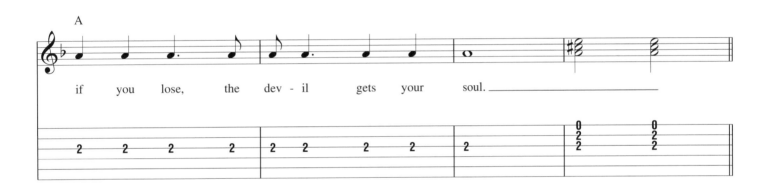

if you lose, the dev - il gets your soul. _____

Interlude

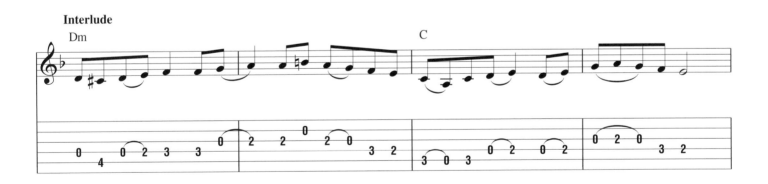

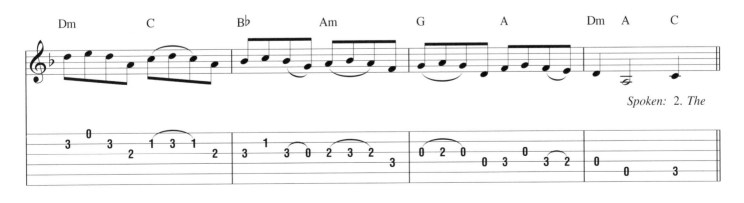

Spoken: 2. The

Verse

D5

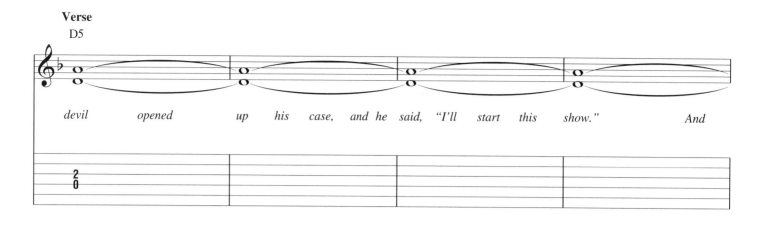

devil opened up his case, and he said, "I'll start this show." And

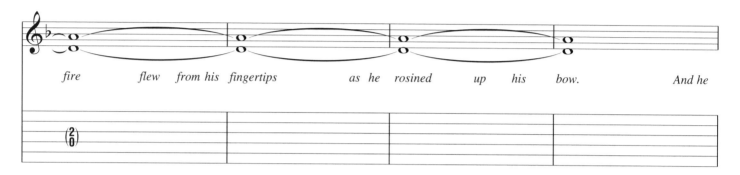

fire flew from his fingertips as he rosined up his bow. And he

N.C.

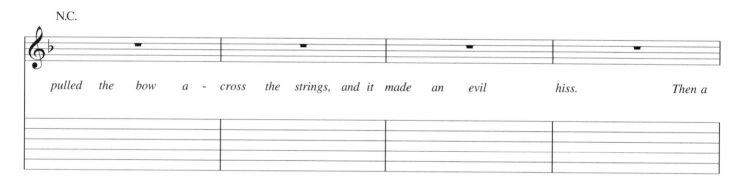

pulled the bow a - cross the strings, and it made an evil hiss. Then a

A   C

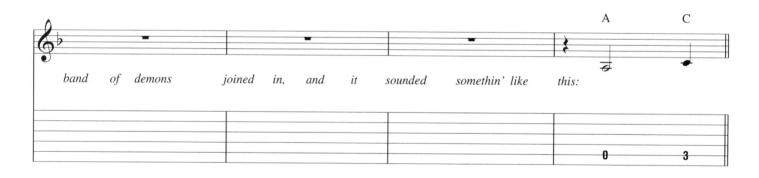

band of demons joined in, and it sounded somethin' like this:

Dm   F/D   Em/D   Dm

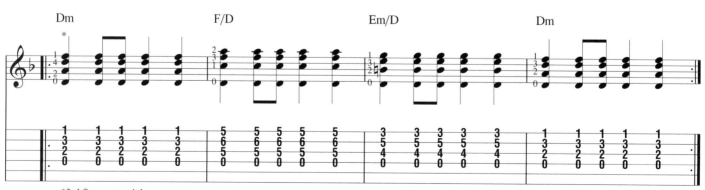

*3rd finger, not pinky, on repeat.

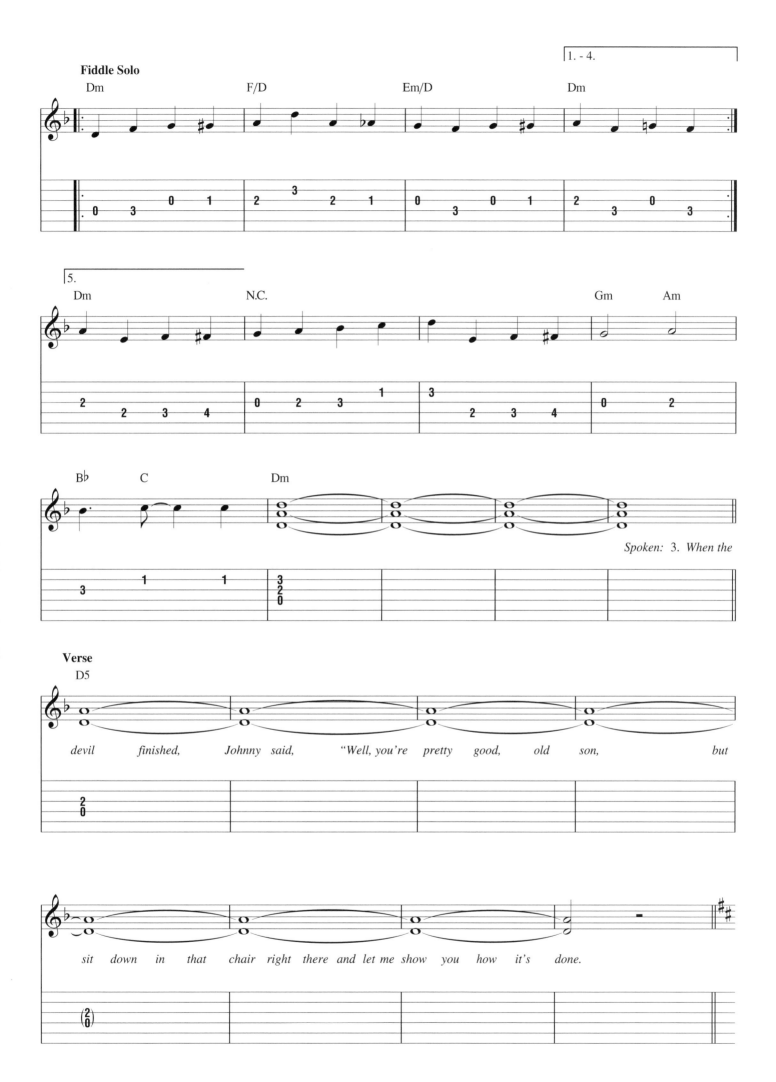

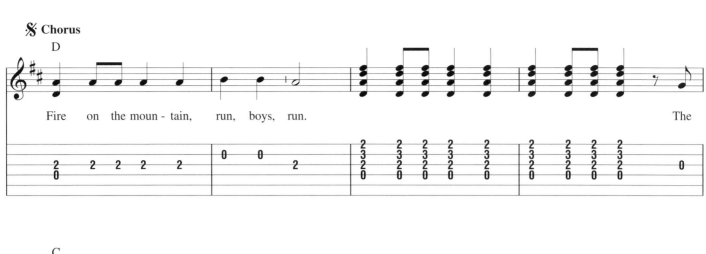

Fire on the moun-tain, run, boys, run. The

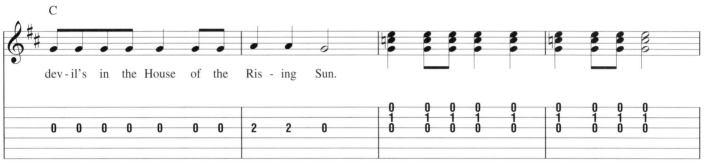

dev-il's in the House of the Ris-ing Sun.

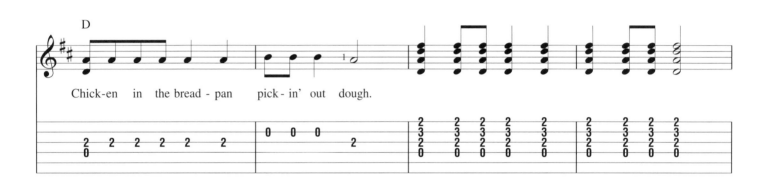

Chick-en in the bread-pan pick-in' out dough.

To Coda ⊕

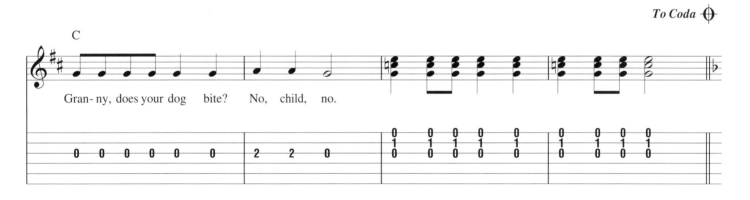

Gran-ny, does your dog bite? No, child, no.

1., 2.

Fiddle Solo

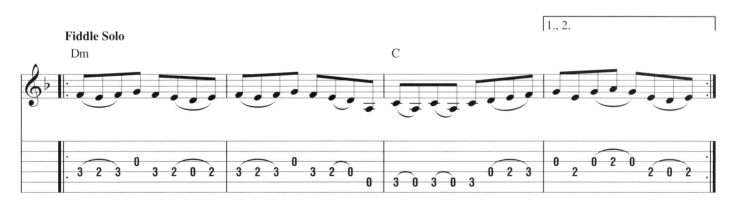

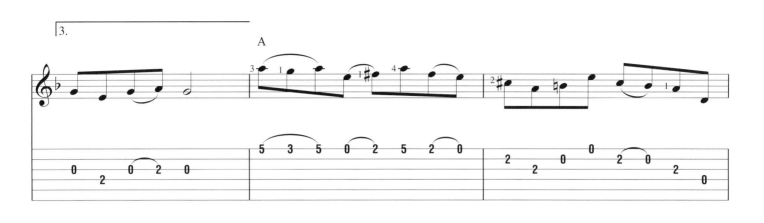

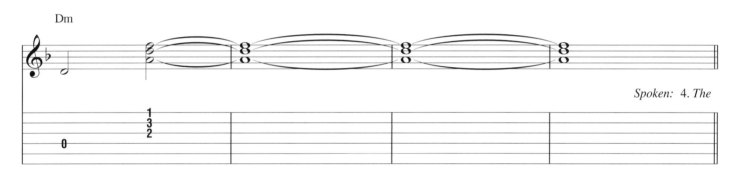

Spoken: 4. *The*

Verse

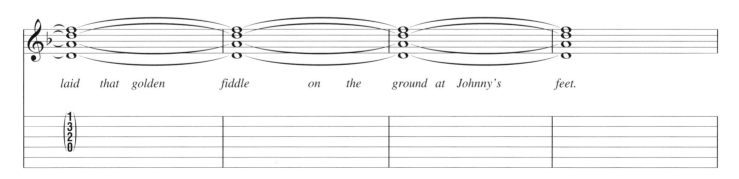

devil   bowed   his   head   because   he   knew   that   he'd   been   beat.   And he

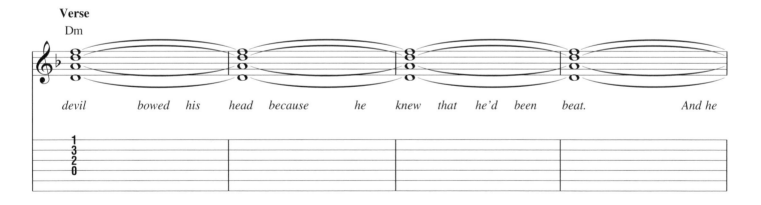

laid   that   golden   fiddle   on   the   ground   at   Johnny's   feet.

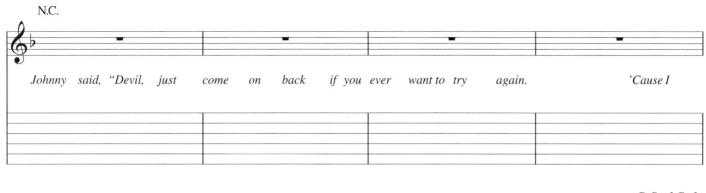

Johnny said, "Devil, just come on back if you ever want to try again.   *'Cause I*

D.S. al Coda

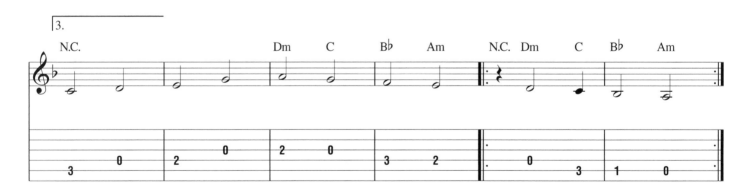

told you once, you son of a gun, I'm the best that's ever been."   He played

⊕ **Coda**

Outro-Fiddle Solo

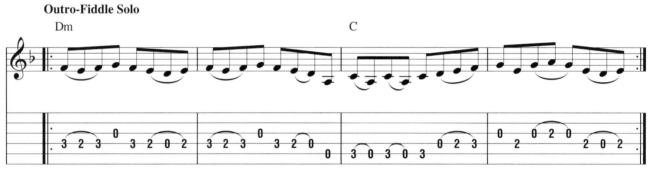

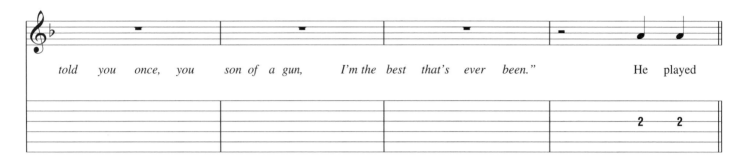

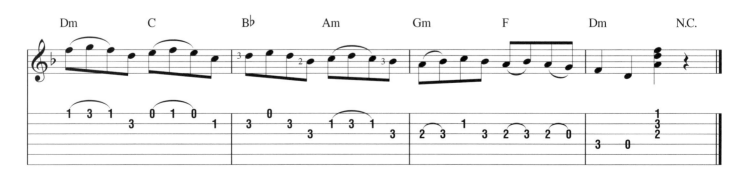

Hold On Loosely

Words and Music by Jeff Carlisi, Don Barnes and Jim Peterik

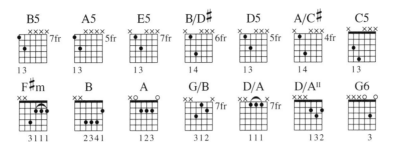

Strum Pattern: 1, 6

Intro
Moderate Rock

1., 3. You see it all a - round you, ___
2. It's so damn eas - 'ly,

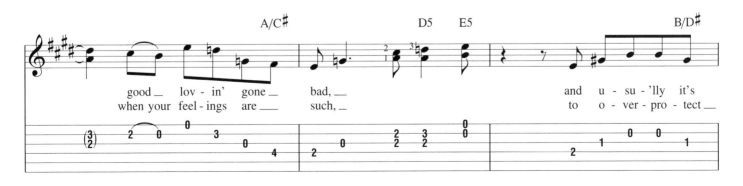

good ___ lov - in' gone ___ bad, ___ and u - su - 'lly it's
when your feel - ings are ___ such, ___ to o - ver - pro - tect ___

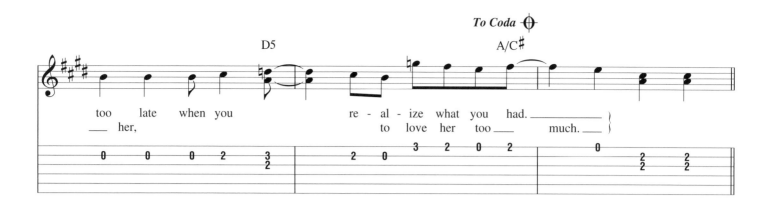

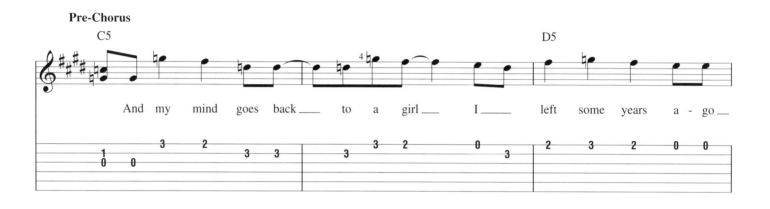

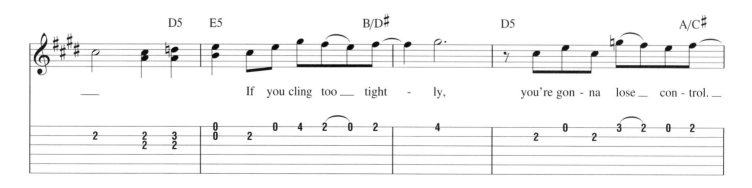

Your ba - by needs some - one to be - lieve in ___

and a whole lot of space ___ to breathe in. ___ ___ to breathe in. ___ ___

*2nd time, let chord ring.

Bridge

Don't let her slip a - way.

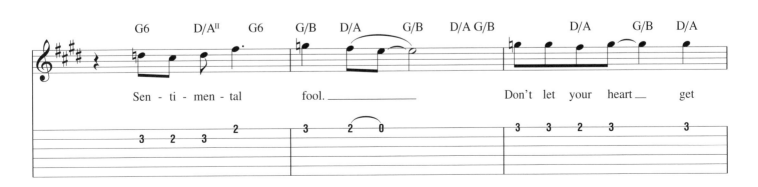

Sen - ti - men - tal fool. ___ Don't let your heart ___ get

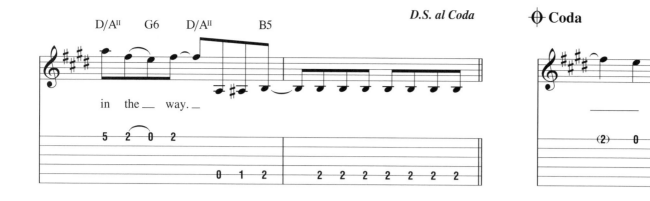

Coda

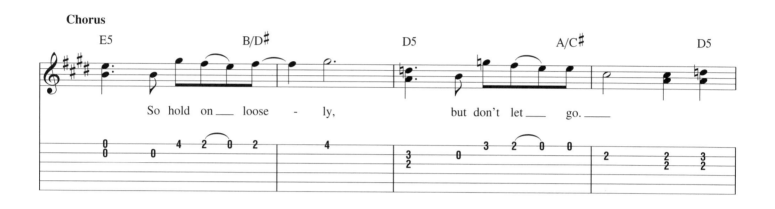

Chorus

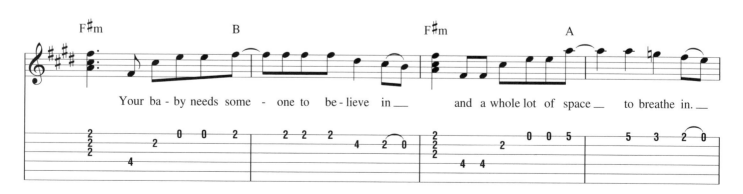

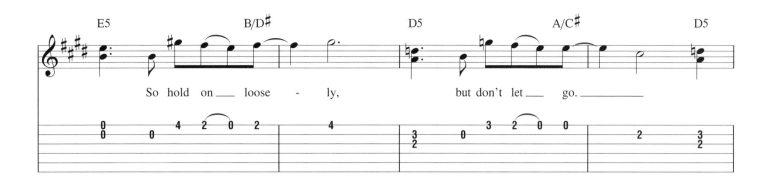

So hold on ___ loose - ly, but don't let ___ go. ___

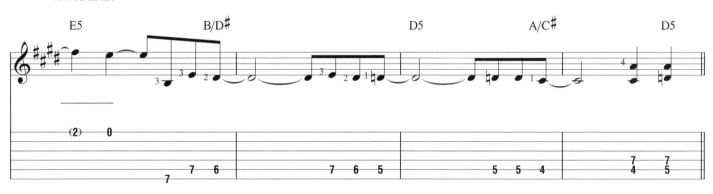

If you cling too ___ tight - ly, you're gon-na lose ___ it. you're gon - na lose con - trol. ___

Outro-Guitar Solo
w/ Voc. ad lib.

Repeat and fade

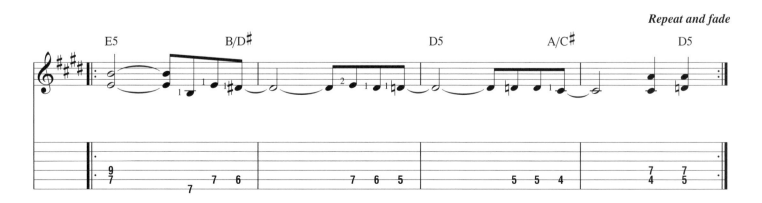

Green Grass and High Tides

Words and Music by Hugh Thomasson Jr.

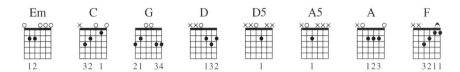

Strum Pattern: 3, 4
Pick Pattern: 3, 4

Intro
Moderate Rock

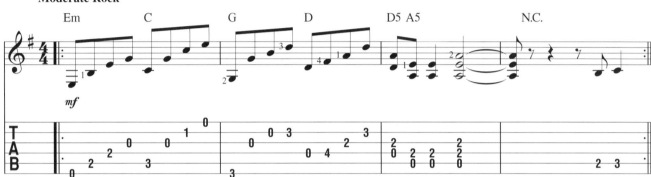

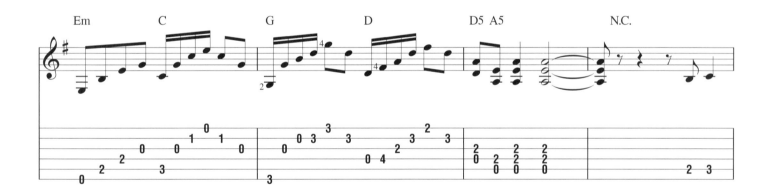

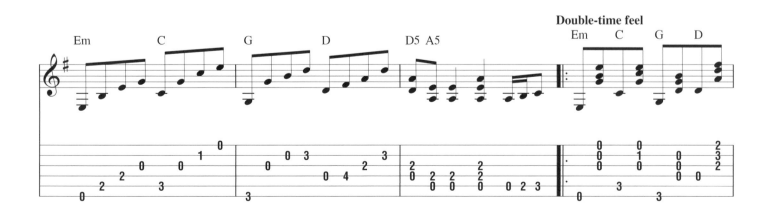

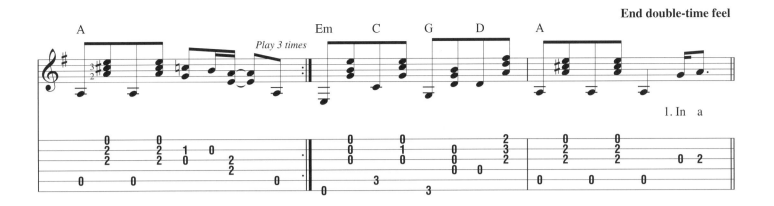

Play 3 times

1. In a

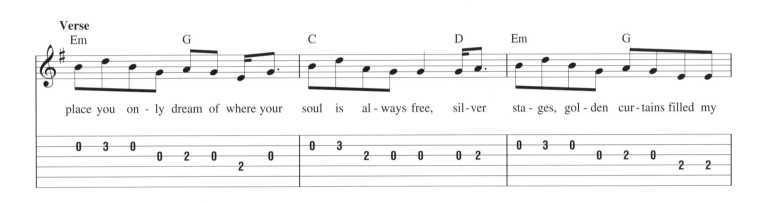

Verse

place you on-ly dream of where your soul is al-ways free, sil-ver sta-ges, gol-den cur-tains filled my

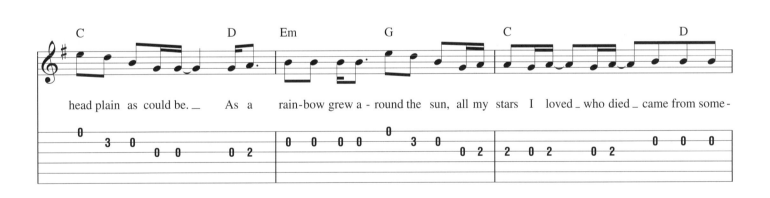

head plain as could be. _ As a rain-bow grew a-round the sun, all my stars I loved _ who died _ came from some-

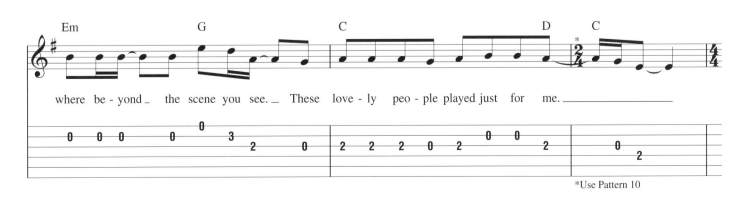

where be-yond _ the scene you see. _ These love-ly peo-ple played just for me. _____

*Use Pattern 10

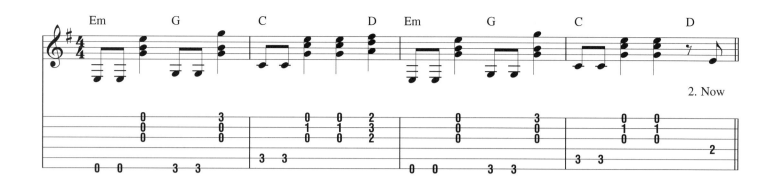

2. Now

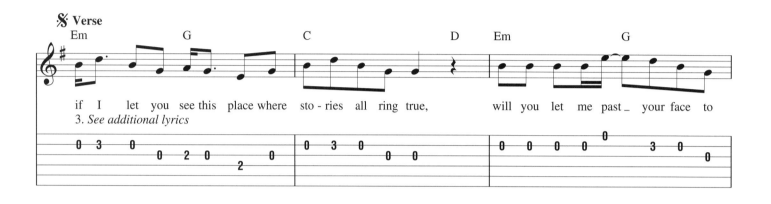

𝄋 Verse

if I let you see this place where sto - ries all ring true, will you let me past _ your face to

3. See additional lyrics

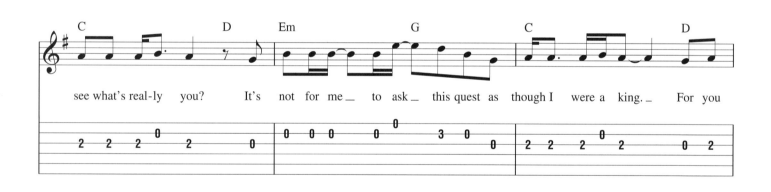

see what's real-ly you? It's not for me _ to ask _ this quest as though I were a king. _ For you

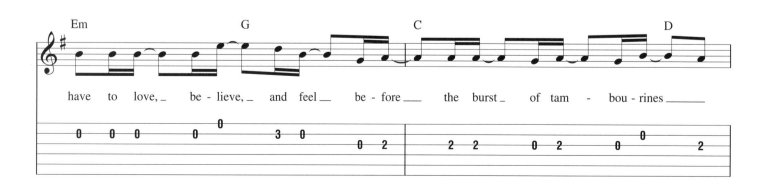

have to love, _ be - lieve, _ and feel _ be - fore _ the burst _ of tam - bou - rines _

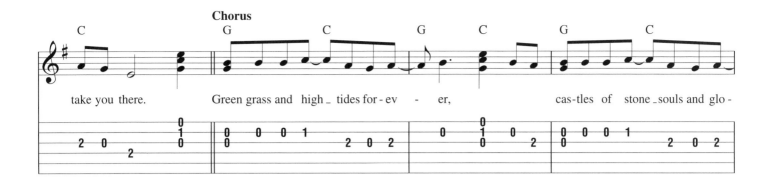

take you there.   Green grass and high _ tides for - ev - _ er,   cas-tles of   stone _ souls and glo -

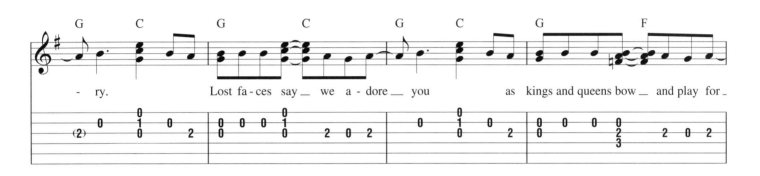

- ry.   Lost fa - ces say _ we a - dore _ you   as   kings and queens bow _ and play for _

To Coda ⊕

Guitar Solo

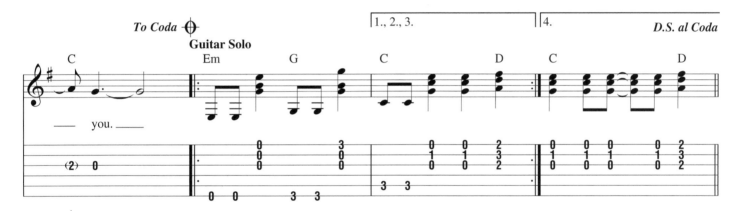

_ you. _

⊕ **Coda**

Outro-Guitar Solo
Double-time feel

Play 4 times

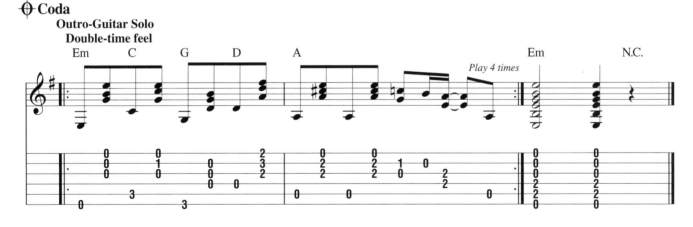

Additional Lyrics

3. Those who don't believe me
Find your souls and set them free.
Those who do, believe and love
As time will be your key.
Time and time again I've thanked them
For a peace of mind.
They helped me find myself amongst
The music and the rhyme
That enchants you there.

If You Want to Get to Heaven

Words and Music by Steve Cash and John Dillon

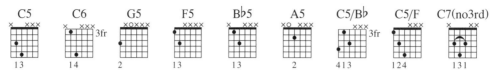

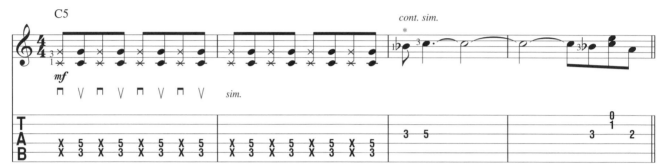

Strum Pattern: 1
Pick Pattern: 5

Intro
Moderate Rock

*Harmonica arr. for gtr., next 4 1/2 meas.

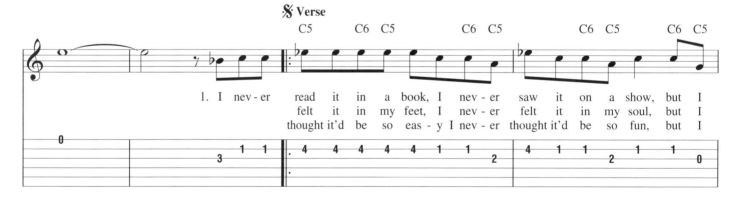

**Synth. arr. for gtr., next 4 1/2 meas.

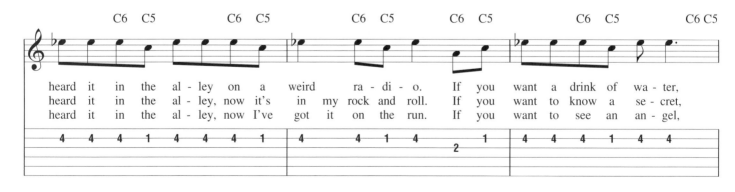

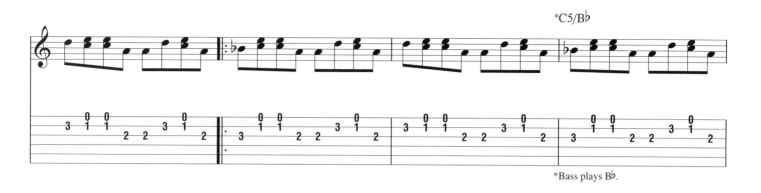

*C5/Bb

*Bass plays Bb.

**C5/F

C5

**Bass plays F.

1.

2.

Outro

C5

If you   want to get to heav-en,   if you

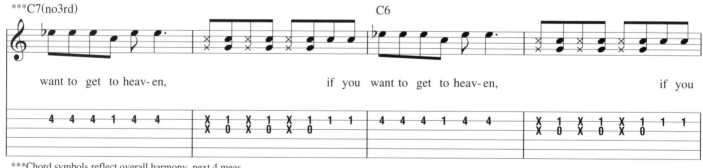

***C7(no3rd)

C6

want to get to heav-en,   if you want to get to heav-en,   if you

***Chord symbols reflect overall harmony, next 4 meas.

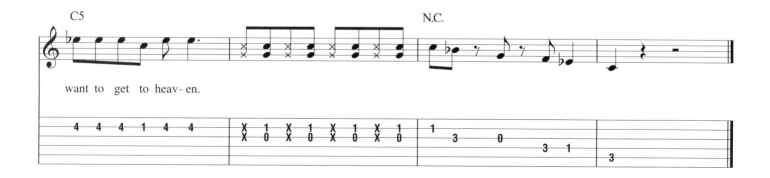

C5

N.C.

want to get to heav-en.

Jim Dandy

Words and Music by Lincoln Chase

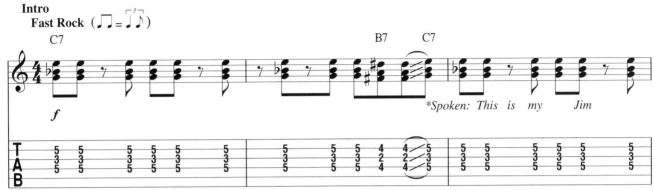

Strum Pattern: 3, 4

Intro
Fast Rock

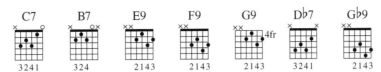

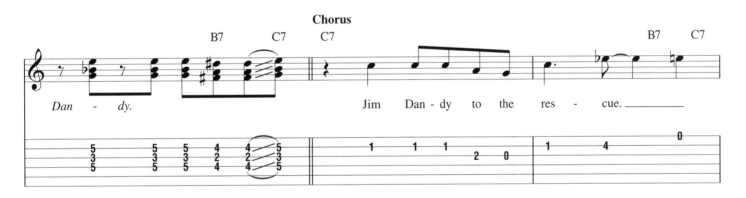

Spoken: This is my Jim

Lyrics in italic are spoken throughout.

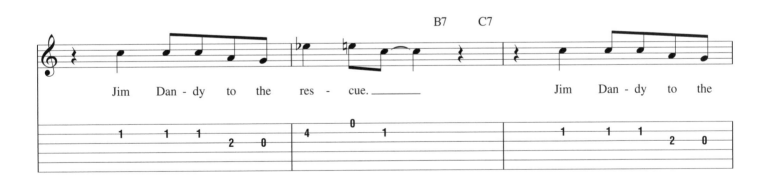

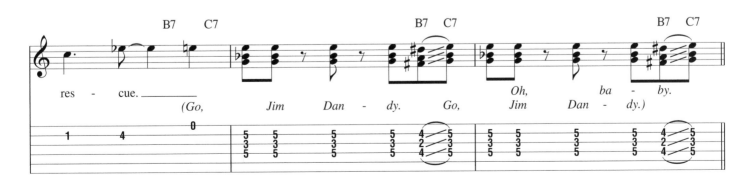

Verse

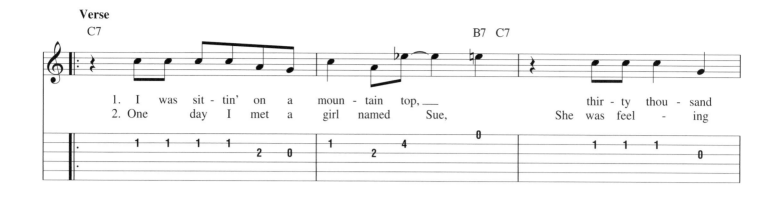

1. I was sit-tin' on a moun-tain top, ___ thir-ty thou-sand
2. One day I met a girl named Sue, She was feel - ing

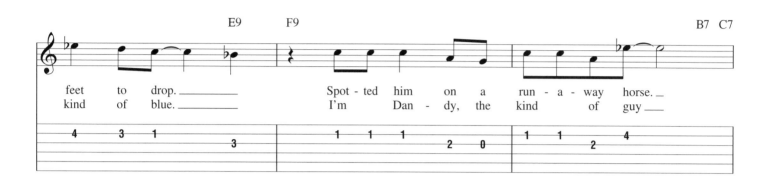

feet to drop. ___ Spot - ted him on a run - a - way horse. ___
kind of blue. ___ I'm Dan - dy, the kind of guy ___

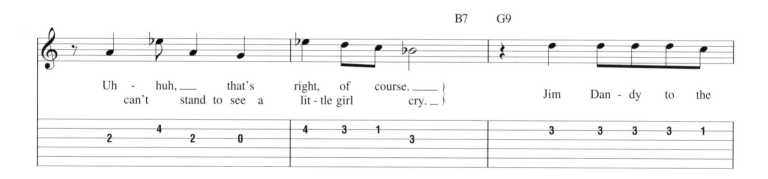

Uh - huh, ___ that's right, of course. ___ } Jim Dan - dy to the
can't stand to see a lit - tle girl cry. ___ }

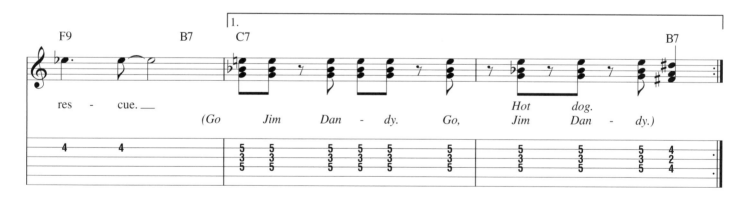

res - cue. ___ (Go Jim Dan - dy. Go, Jim Dan - dy.) _Hot dog._

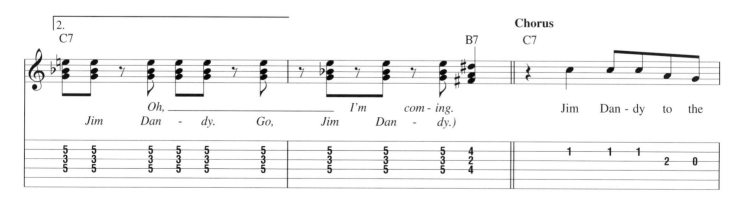

Jim Dan - dy. _Go, Jim Dan - dy.)_ Oh, ___ I'm com - ing. Jim Dan - dy to the

res - cue. _____ Jim Dan - dy to the res - cue. _____

Jim Dan - dy to the res - cue. _____

(Go, Jim Dan - dy, go!)

Guitar Solo

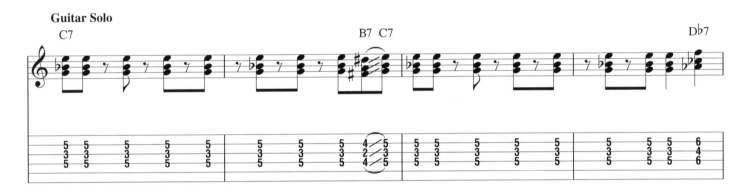

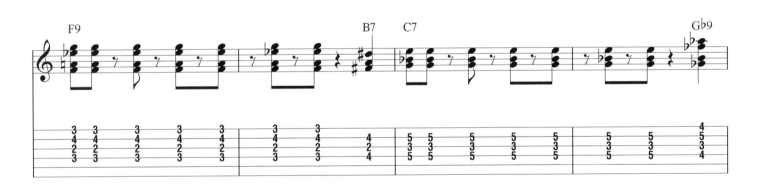

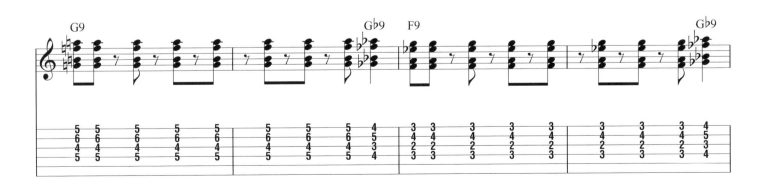

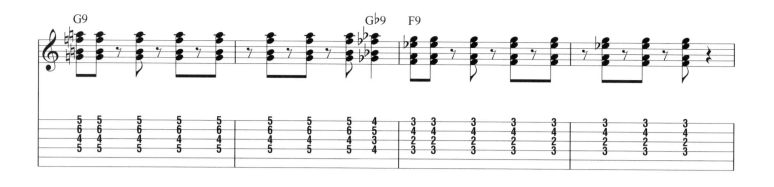

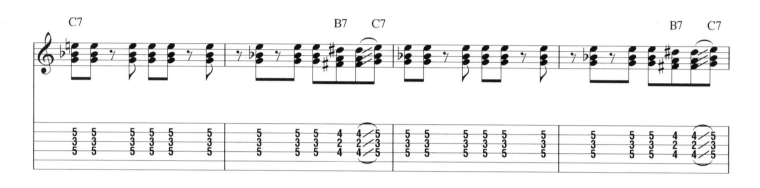

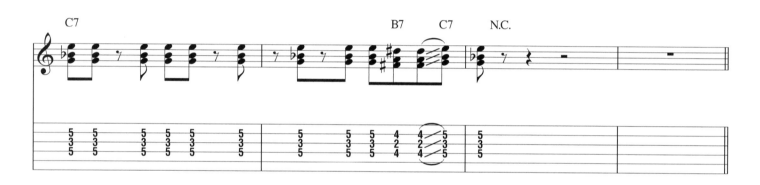

Verse

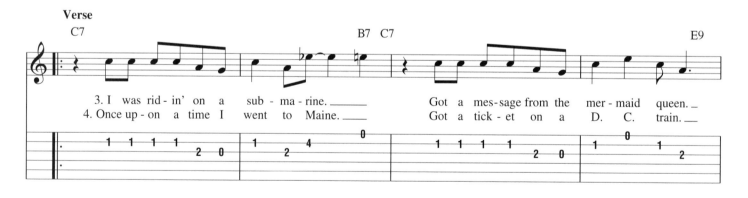

3. I was rid-in' on a sub-ma-rine. _____ Got a mes-sage from the mer-maid queen. _
4. Once up-on a time I went to Maine. _____ Got a tick-et on a D. C. train. _

She was hang - ing on my fish-ing line. _____ This Dan-dy did-n't waste no time. _
This Dan-dy did-n't need no chute. _____ I was high _____ and read-y to boot. _

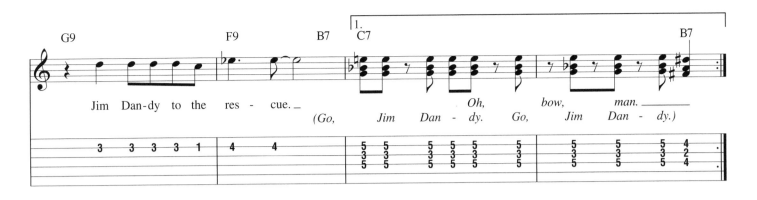

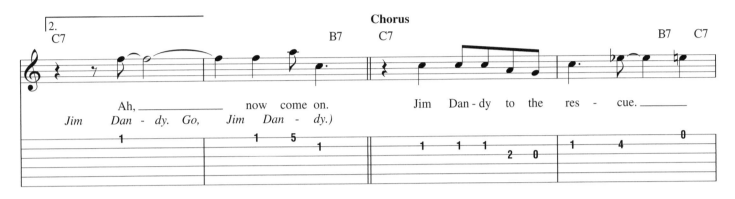

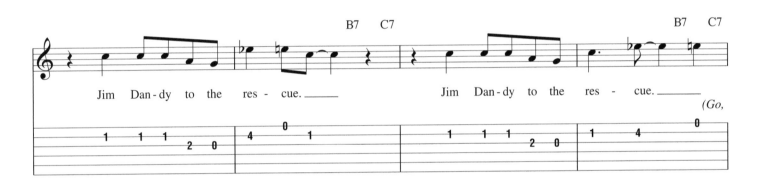

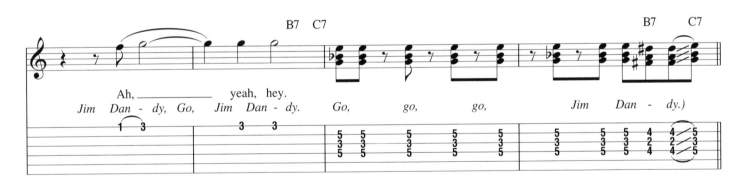

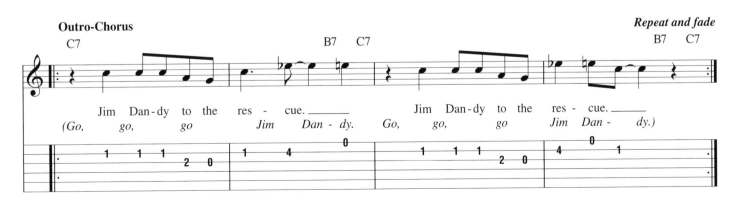

Jackie Blue

Words and Music by Larry Lee and Steve Cash

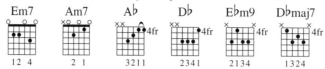

Em7   Am7   A♭   D♭   E♭m9   D♭maj7

*Tune down 1/2 step:
(low to high) E♭-A♭-D♭-G♭-B♭-E♭

Strum Pattern: 2, 3
Pick Pattern: 3, 4

Intro
Moderately

S: **Chorus**

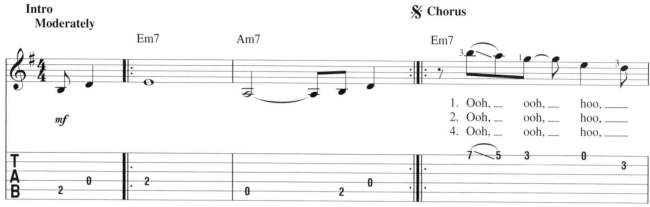

1. Ooh, __ ooh, __ hoo, ____
2. Ooh, __ ooh, __ hoo, ____
4. Ooh, __ ooh, __ hoo, ____

*Optional: To match recording, tune down 1/2 step.

Jack - ie Blue   lives her life __ from in - side of a room.
Jack - ie Blue,   what's a game, __ girl, if you nev - er lose?
Jack - ie Blue   lives a dream __ that can nev - er come true.

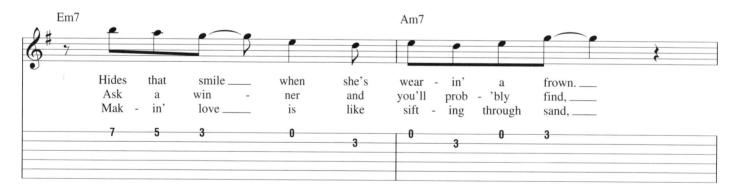

Hides that smile ____ when she's wear - in' a frown. ____
Ask a win - ner and you'll prob - 'bly find, ____
Mak - in' love ____ is like sift - ing through sand, ____

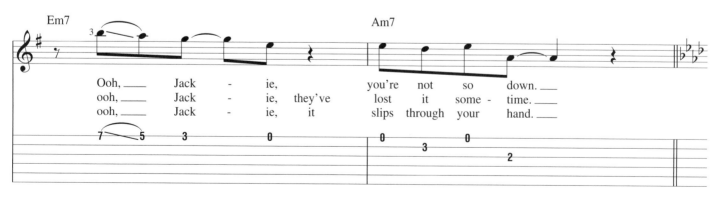

Ooh, ____ Jack - ie, you're not so down. ____
ooh, ____ Jack - ie, they've lost it some - time. ____
ooh, ____ Jack - ie, it slips through your hand. ____

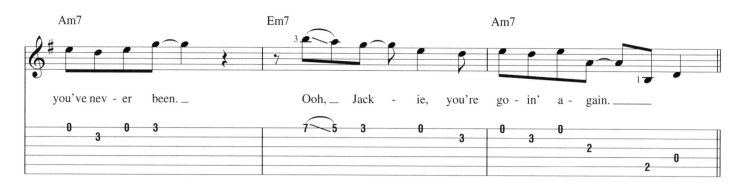

you've nev - er been. __ Ooh, __ Jack - ie, you're go - in' a - gain. _____

Guitar Solo

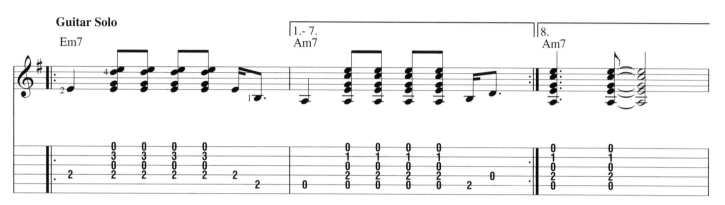

D.S. al Coda

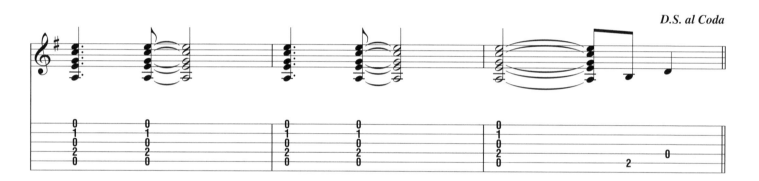

⊕ Coda

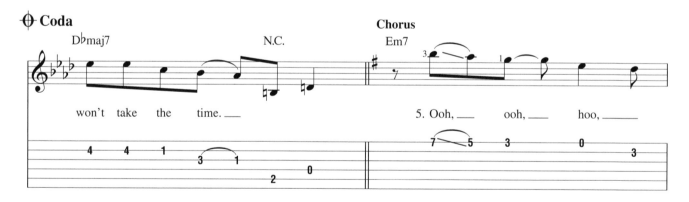

won't take the time. ___

Chorus

5. Ooh, ___ ooh, ___ hoo, _____

Jack - ie Blue, lives her life ___ from in - side of a room. __

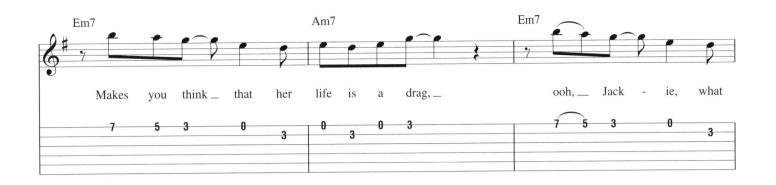

Makes you think __ that her life is a drag, __ ooh, __ Jack - ie, what

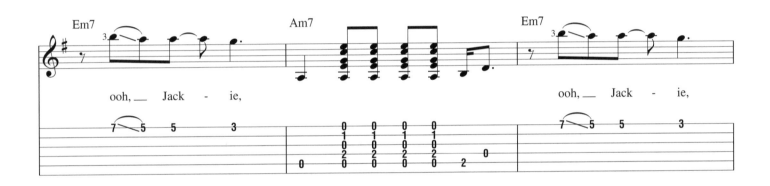

fun you have had. __ Ooh, __ Jack - ie,

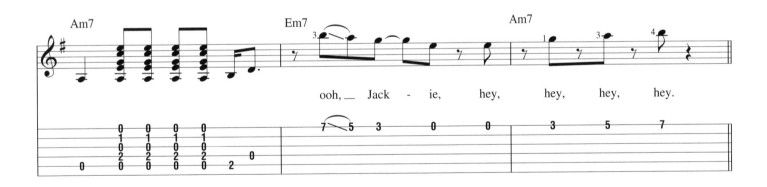

ooh, __ Jack - ie, ooh, __ Jack - ie,

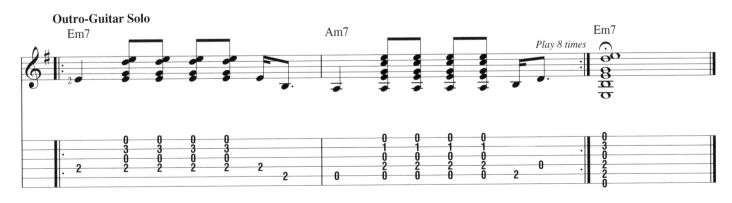

ooh, __ Jack - ie, hey, hey, hey, hey.

Outro-Guitar Solo

Play 8 times

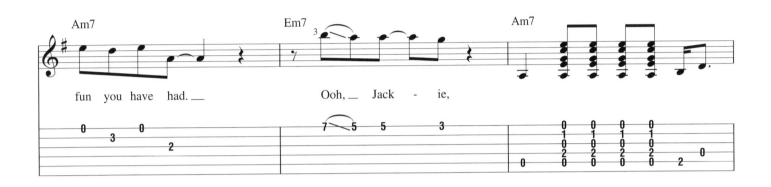

Midnight Rider

Words and Music by Gregg Allman and Robert Kim Payne

Strum Pattern: 3, 6
Pick Pattern: 2

Additional Lyrics

2. And I don't own the clothes I'm wearin'.
   And the road goes on forever.
   And I've got one more silver dollar.

3. And I'm gone past the point of carin'.
   Some ol' bed I'll soon be sharin',
   And I've got one more silver dollar.

Mississippi Queen

Words and Music by Leslie West, Felix Pappalardi, Corky Laing and David Rea

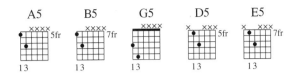

Strum Pattern: 4
Pick Pattern: 3

Intro
Moderately

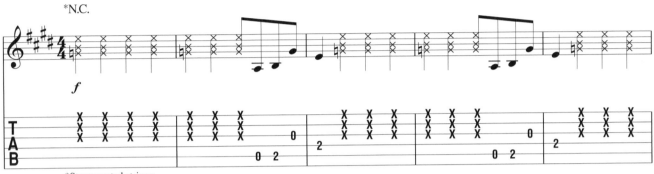

*Strum muted strings.

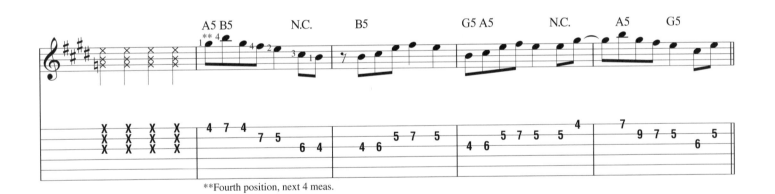

**Fourth position, next 4 meas.

1, 2. Mis-sis-sip-pi   Queen, _

3. *Instrumental*

{do you know _ what I   mean?}
{if you know _ what I   mean.}

***Sung one octave higher throughout.

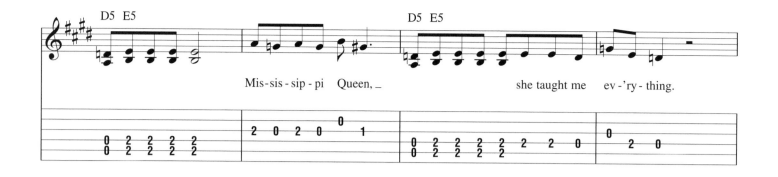

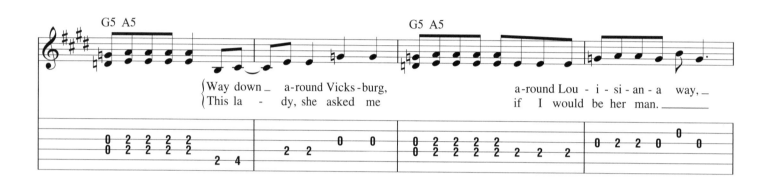

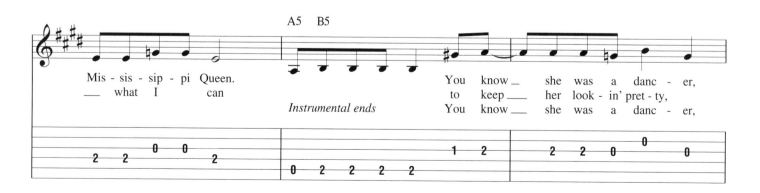

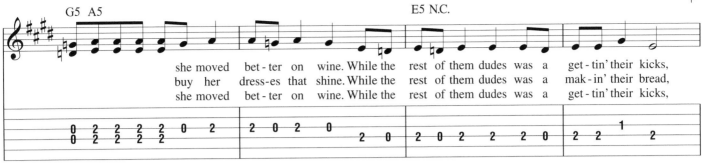

she moved — bet - ter on — wine. While the rest of them dudes was a get - tin' their kicks,
buy her — dress-es that shine. While the rest of them dudes was a mak - in' their bread,
she moved — bet - ter on — wine. While the rest of them dudes was a get - tin' their kicks,

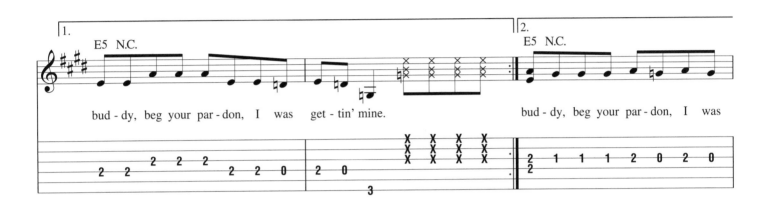

bud - dy, beg your par - don, I was get - tin' mine.

bud - dy, beg your par - don, I was

⊕ **Coda**

D.S. al Coda

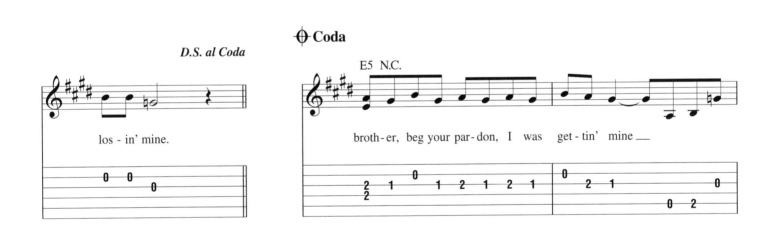

los - in' mine.

broth - er, beg your par - don, I was get - tin' mine —

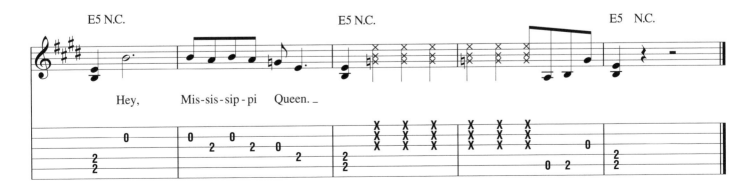

Hey, Mis-sis-sip - pi Queen. —

Ramblin' Man

Words and Music by Dickey Betts

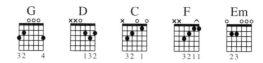

Strum Pattern: 6
Pick Pattern: 4

Intro
Fast Rock

Chorus

Lord, I ___ was born a ram - blin' man. ___

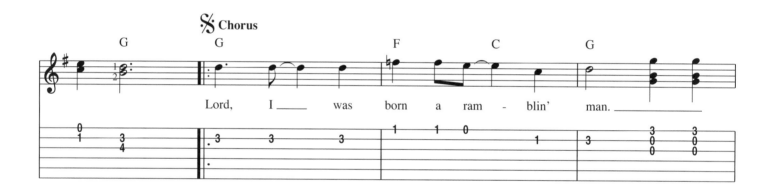

Try'n to make a liv - ing, and do - in' the best I ___

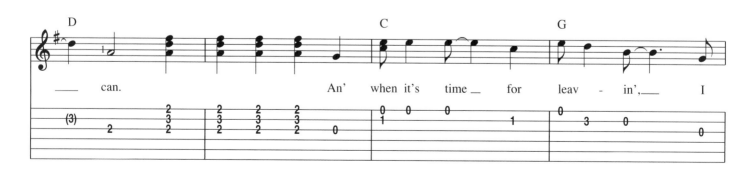

___ can. An' when it's time __ for leav - in', ___ I

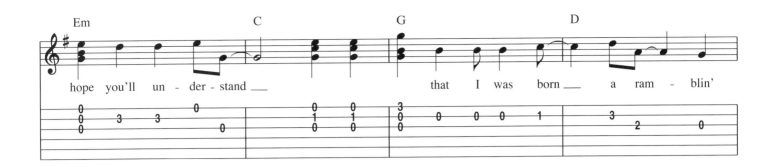

hope you'll un - der - stand ___ that I was born ___ a ram - blin'

To Coda ⊕ **Verse**

man. 1. Well, my fath - er was ___ a gam - bler down in
2. *See additional lyrics*

Geor - gia, ___ and he wound up on ___ the wrong ___

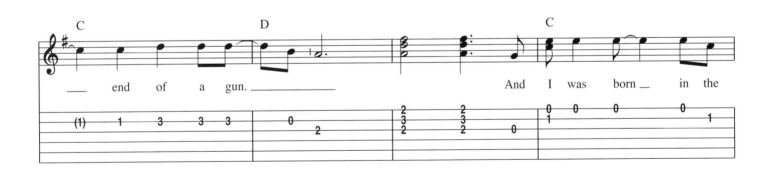

___ end of a gun. ___ And I was born ___ in the

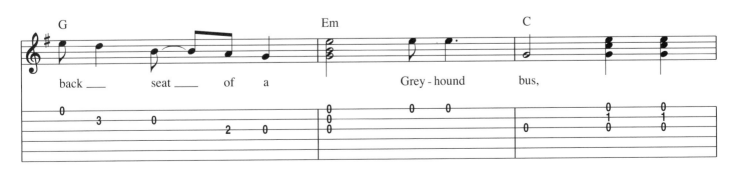

back ___ seat ___ of a Grey - hound bus,

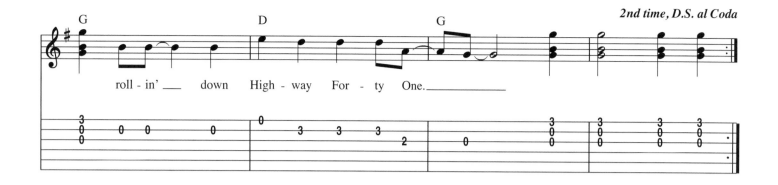

roll - in' ___ down High - way For - ty One. _____

Coda

Outro

Lord, I ____ was born a ram - blin'

man. _____ Lord, I _____ was

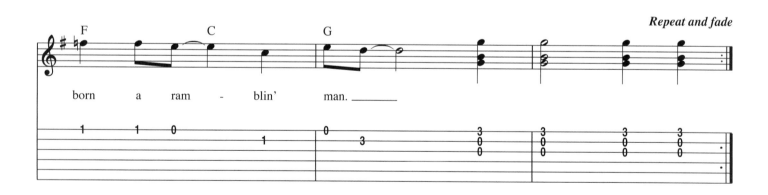

born a ram - blin' man. _____

Additional Lyrics

2. I'm on my way to New Orleans this mornin',
And leavin' out of Nashville, Tennessee.
They're always havin' a good time down on the bayou, Lord.
Them delta women think the world of me.

Rockin' Into the Night

Words and Music by Frank Sullivan, Robert Smith and Jim Peterik

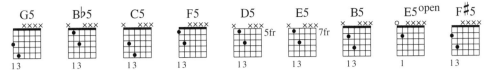

Strum Pattern: 3, 4

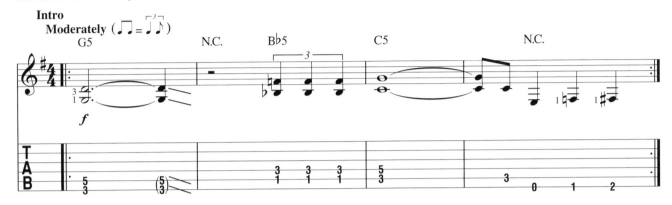

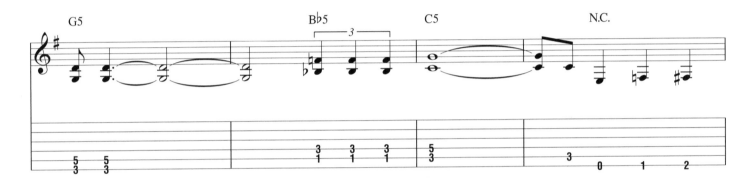

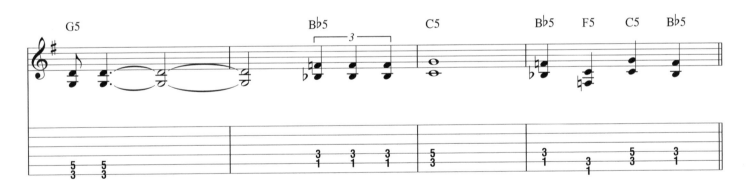

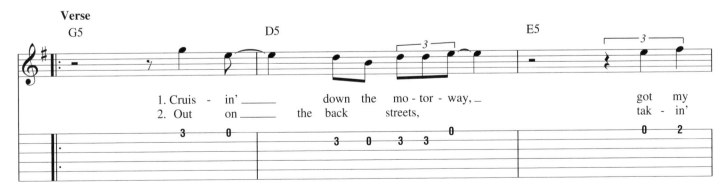

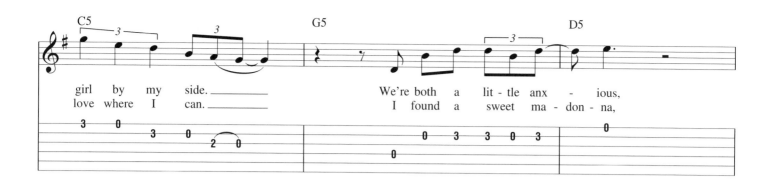

℈ Pre-Chorus

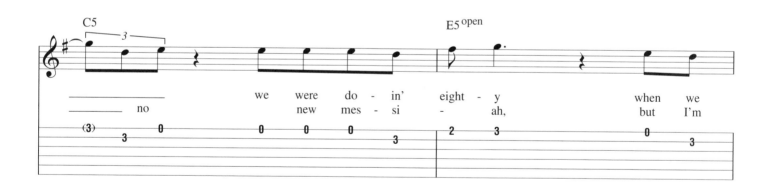

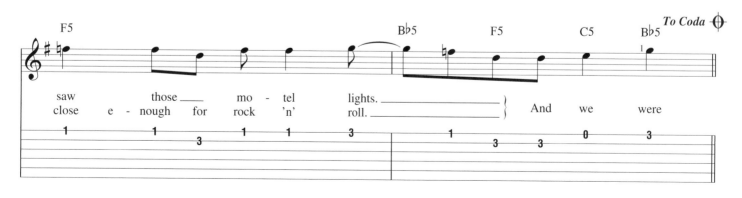

Susie-Q

Words and Music by Dale Hawkins, Stan Lewis and Eleanor Broadwater

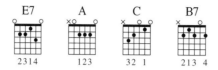

Strum Pattern: 4
Pick Pattern: 1, 4

Intro
Moderately

1., 5. Oh, __ Su - sie - Q. __   Oh, __ Su - sie - Q. __
3. *See additional lyrics*

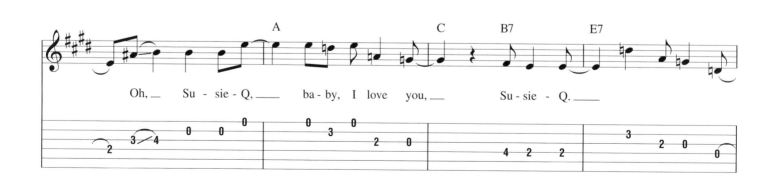

Oh, __ Su - sie - Q, __ ba - by, I love you, __ Su - sie - Q. __

Verse

2. Like the way   you   walk. ___   I   like the way   you   talk. ___
4. *See additional lyrics*

To Coda 2 ⊕

I   like the way   you   walk, ___   I   like the way   you   talk, ___   Su - sie - Q. ___

To Coda 1 ⊕
Guitar Solo

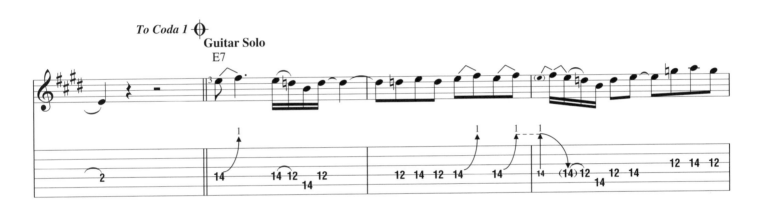

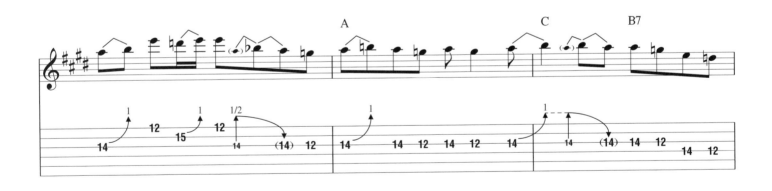

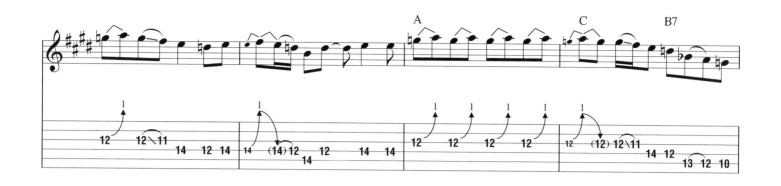

⊕ Coda 1

D.C. al Coda 1
(take repeat)

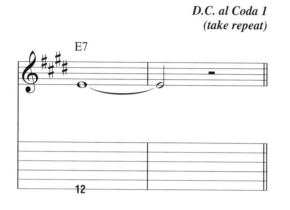

Guitar Solo

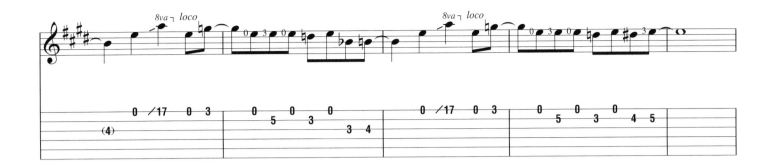

D.C. al Coda 2
(take repeat)

⊕ Coda 2

Verse

6. Oh, Su-sie - Q. ____

Oh, Su-sie - Q. ____   Oh, Su-sie - Q, ____ ba-by, I love you, ____ Su-sie - Q. ____

Outro   *Repeat and fade*

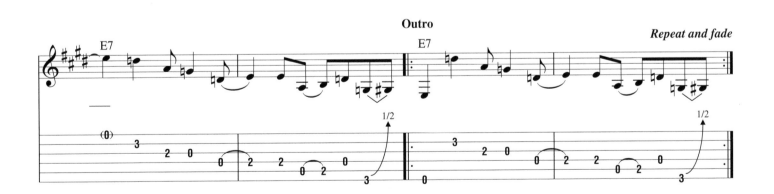

Additional Lyrics

3. Well, say that you'll be true.
   Well, say that you'll be true.
   Well, say that you'll be true
   And never leave me blue, Susie-Q.

4. Well, say that you'll be mine.
   Well, say that you'll be mine.
   Well, say that you'll be mine,
   Baby, all the time, Susie-Q.

Sweet Home Alabama

Words and Music by Ronnie Van Zant, Ed King and Gary Rossington

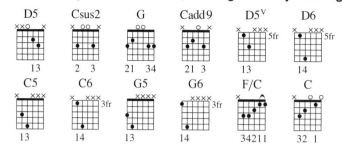

Strum Pattern: 2
Pick Pattern: 4

Intro
Moderately

Spoken: Turn it up.

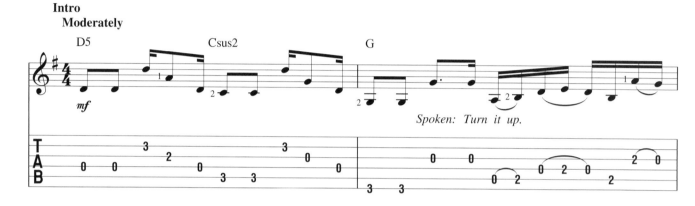

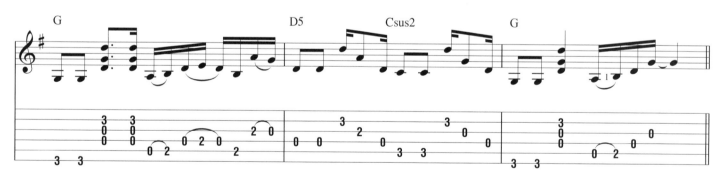

Verse

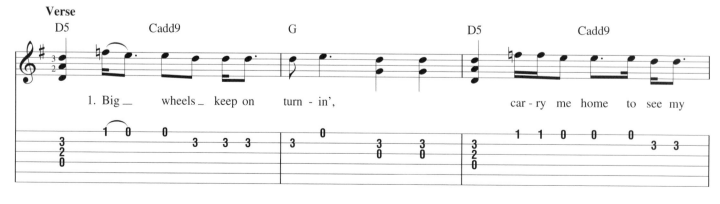

1. Big wheels keep on turn-in', car-ry me home to see my

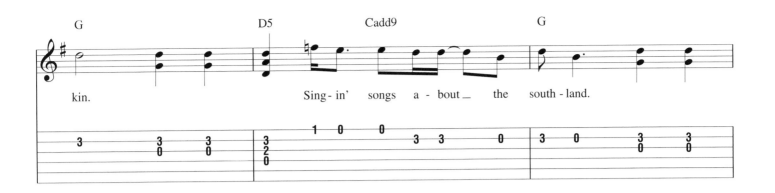

kin. Sing-in' songs a-bout__ the south-land.

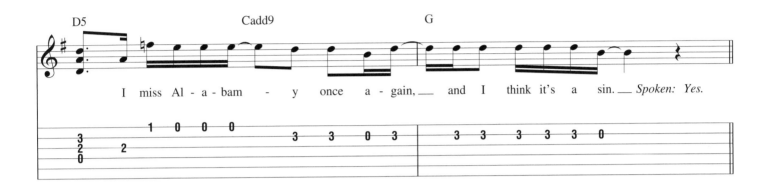

I miss Al-a-bam — y once a-gain,__ and I think it's a sin. __ *Spoken: Yes.*

Interlude

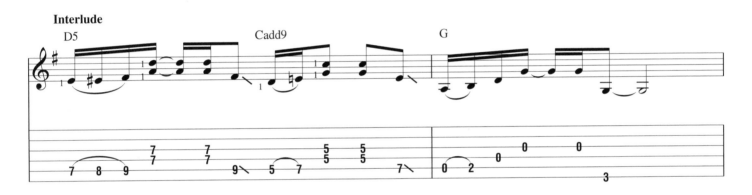

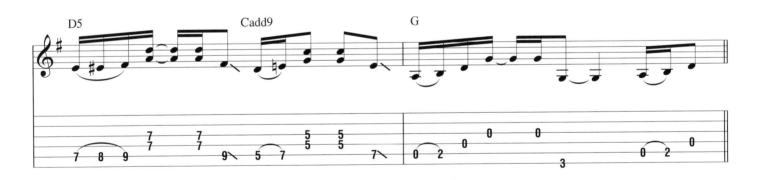

𝄋 **Verse**

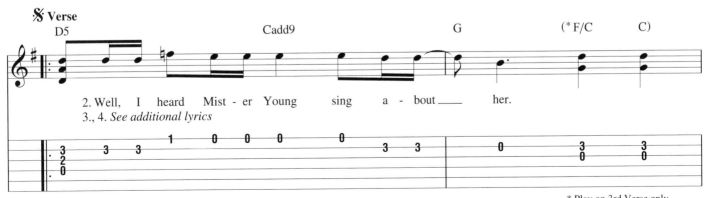

2. Well, I heard Mist-er Young sing a-bout____ her.
3., 4. *See additional lyrics*

* Play on 3rd Verse only

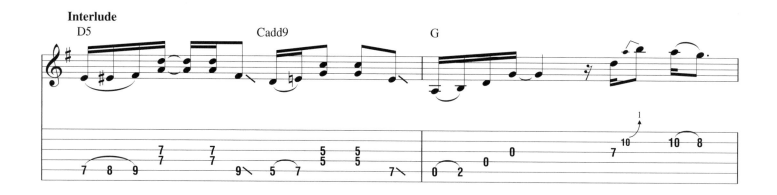

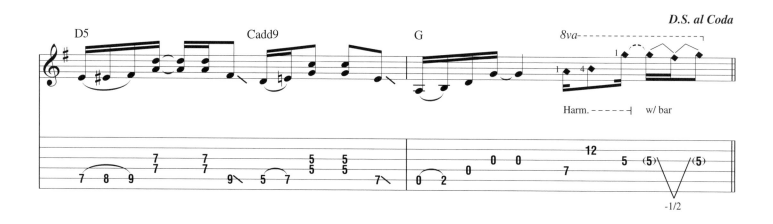

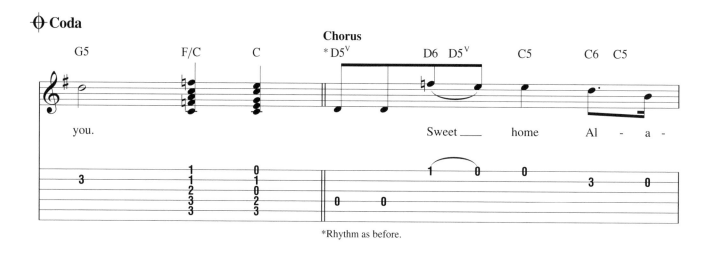

*Rhythm as before.

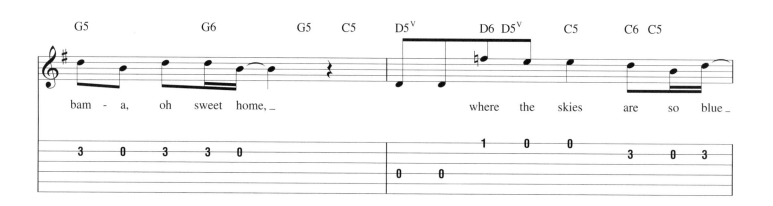

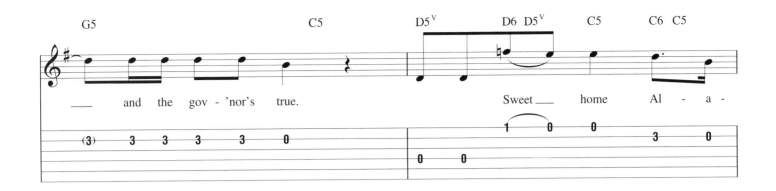

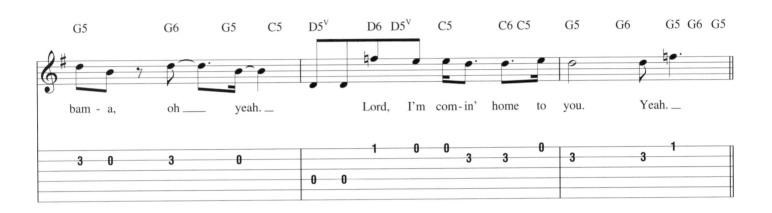

Outro

Repeat and fade

* Yeah.

* 1st time only.

Additional Lyrics

3. In Birmingham they love the gov'nor. Boo, boo, boo.
   Now we all did what we could do.
   Now Watergate does not bother me,
   Does your conscience bother you? Tell the truth.

4. Now Muscle Shoals has got the Swampers,
   An' they been known to pick a song or two. (Yes they do!)
   Lord, they get me off so much,
   They pick me up when I'm feelin' blue 'n' now how 'bout you?

Train, Train

Words and Music by Shorty Medlocke

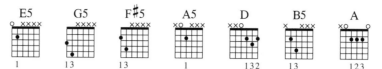

Strum Pattern: 2, 3

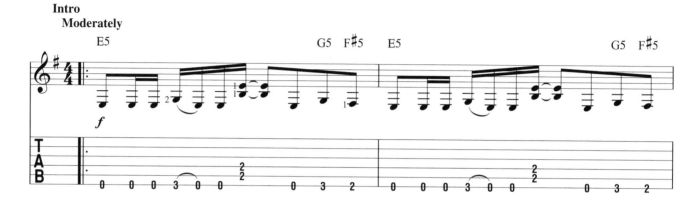

Spoken: Oh, _____ here it comes!

1. Well, train,
   leav - in'
   good - bye, _____ pret-ty

train,
here,
ma - ma,

I'm just a
get _____ your - self

take _____ me on out _____ of _____ this
rag - ged - y _____ ho - bo. _____
a mon - ey man.

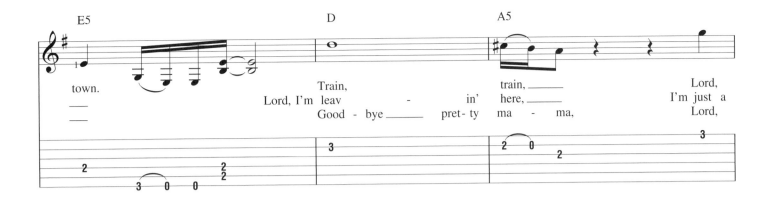

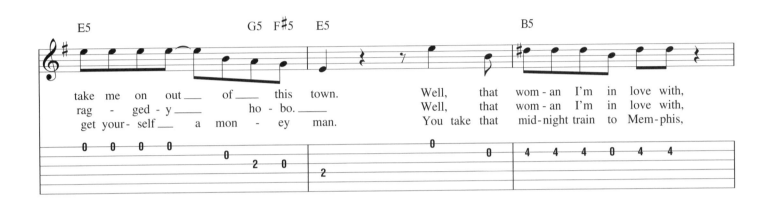

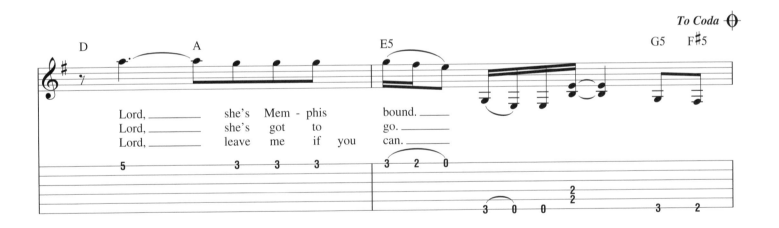

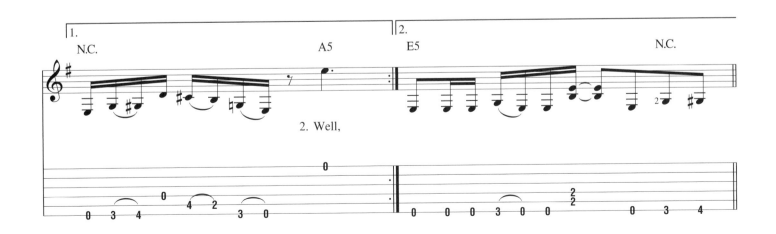

Coda

Oh, ____ take that mid-night train to Mem-phis,

Lord, _____ leave me if you can. _____

Guitar Solo

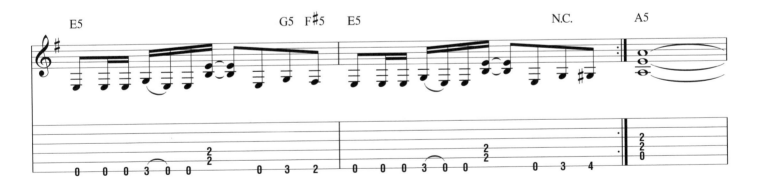

(Drum fill)

There Goes Another Love Song

Words and Music by Hugh Thomasson Jr. and Byron Yoho

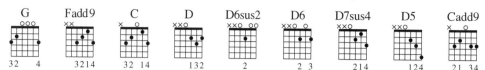

G   Fadd9   C   D   D6sus2   D6   D7sus4   D5   Cadd9

Strum Pattern: 3, 5
Pick Pattern: 3, 4

Intro
Moderately fast Rock

Play 3 times

mf

% Verse

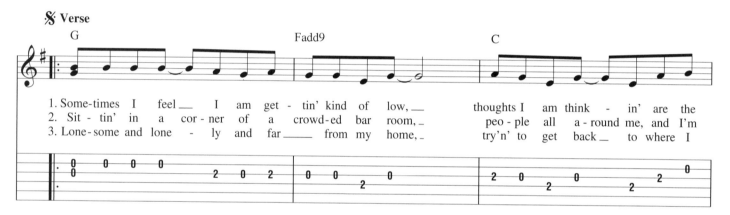

1. Some-times I feel ___ I am get - tin' kind of low, ___ thoughts I am think - in' are the
2. Sit - tin' in a cor - ner of a crowd-ed bar room, _ peo - ple all a - round me, and I'm
3. Lone-some and lone - ly and far ___ from my home, _ try'n' to get back ___ to where I

rea - son, ___ so ___ I try to re - mem - ber, with - out talk - in' to my - self,
still feel - in' low. ___ Just when I know ___ I'm gon - na break down and cry, ___
know I be - long. ___ Wish-in' and I'm hop - in' I was al - read - y there, _

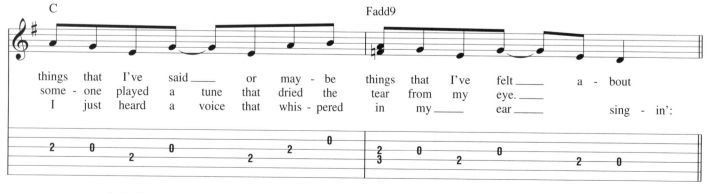

things that I've said ___ or may - be things that I've felt ___ a - bout
some - one played a tune that dried the tear from my eye. ___
I just heard a voice that whis - pered in my ___ ear ___ sing - in':

© 1975 (Renewed 2003) HUSTLER'S INC. (BMI)/Administered by BUG MUSIC and GUITAR ARMY PUBLISHING
All Rights Reserved Used by Permission

EASY GUITAR
WITH NOTES & TAB

This series features simplified arrangements with notes, tab, chord charts, and strum and pick patterns.

MIXED FOLIOS

00702002	Acoustic Rock Hits for Easy Guitar	$12.95
00702166	All-Time Best Guitar Collection	$19.99
00699665	Beatles Best	$12.95
00702232	Best Acoustic Songs for Easy Guitar	$12.99
00702233	Best Hard Rock Songs	$14.99
00698978	Big Christmas Collection	$16.95
00702115	Blues Classics	$10.95
00385020	Broadway Songs for Kids	$9.95
00702237	Christian Acoustic Favorites	$12.95
00702149	Children's Christian Songbook	$7.95
00702028	Christmas Classics	$7.95
00702185	Christmas Hits	$9.95
00702016	Classic Blues for Easy Guitar	$12.95
00702141	Classic Rock	$8.95
00702203	CMT's 100 Greatest Country Songs	$27.95
00702170	Contemporary Christian Christmas	$9.95
00702006	Contemporary Christian Favorites	$9.95
00702065	Contemporary Women of Country	$9.95
00702121	Country from the Heart	$9.95
00702240	Country Hits of 2007-2008	$12.95
00702225	Country Hits of '06-'07	$12.95
00702085	Disney Movie Hits	$12.95
00702257	Easy Acoustic Guitar Songs	$14.99
00702212	Essential Christmas	$9.95
00702041	Favorite Hymns for Easy Guitar	$9.95
00702174	God Bless America® & Other Songs for a Better Nation	$8.95
00699374	Gospel Favorites	$14.95
00702160	The Great American Country Songbook	$14.95
00702050	Great Classical Themes for Easy Guitar	$6.95
00702131	Great Country Hits of the '90s	$8.95
00702116	Greatest Hymns for Guitar	$8.95
00702130	The Groovy Years	$9.95
00702184	Guitar Instrumentals	$9.95
00702231	High School Musical for Easy Guitar	$12.95
00702241	High School Musical 2	$12.95
00702249	High School Musical 3	$12.99
00702037	Hits of the '50s for Easy Guitar	$10.95
00702046	Hits of the '70s for Easy Guitar	$8.95
00702032	International Songs for Easy Guitar	$12.95
00702051	Jock Rock for Easy Guitar	$9.95
00702162	Jumbo Easy Guitar Songbook	$19.95
00702112	Latin Favorites	$9.95
00702258	Legends of Rock	$14.99
00702138	Mellow Rock Hits	$10.95
00702147	Motown's Greatest Hits	$9.95
00702039	Movie Themes	$10.95
00702210	Best of MTV Unplugged	$12.95
00702189	MTV's 100 Greatest Pop Songs	$24.95
00702272	1950s Rock	$14.99
00702271	1960s Rock	$14.99
00702270	1970s Rock	$14.99
00702269	1980s Rock	$14.99
00702268	1990s Rock	$14.99
00702187	Selections from O Brother Where Art Thou?	$12.95
00702178	100 Songs for Kids	$12.95
00702158	Songs from Passion	$9.95
00702125	Praise and Worship for Guitar	$9.95
00702155	Rock Hits for Guitar	$9.95
00702242	Rock Band	$19.95
00702256	Rock Band 2	$19.99
00702128	Rockin' Down the Highway	$9.95
00702207	Smash Hits for Guitar	$9.95
00702110	The Sound of Music	$9.99
00702124	Today's Christian Rock – 2nd Edition	$9.95
00702220	Today's Country Hits	$9.95
00702198	Today's Hits for Guitar	$9.95
00702217	Top Christian Hits	$12.95
00702235	Top Christian Hits of '07-'08	$14.95
00702246	Top Hits of 2008	$12.95
00702206	Very Best of Rock	$9.95
00702175	VH1's 100 Greatest Songs of Rock and Roll	$24.95
00702253	Wicked	$12.99
00702192	Worship Favorites	$9.95

ARTIST COLLECTIONS

00702267	AC/DC for Easy Guitar	$14.99
00702001	Best of Aerosmith	$16.95
00702040	Best of the Allman Brothers	$12.95
00702169	Best of The Beach Boys	$10.95
00702201	The Essential Black Sabbath	$12.95
00702140	Best of Brooks & Dunn	$10.95
00702095	Best of Mariah Carey	$12.95
00702043	Best of Johnny Cash	$12.95
00702033	Best of Steven Curtis Chapman	$14.95
00702263	Best of Casting Crowns	$12.99
00702090	Eric Clapton's Best	$10.95
00702086	Eric Clapton – from the Album Unplugged	$10.95
00702202	The Essential Eric Clapton	$12.95
00702250	blink-182 – Greatest Hits	$12.99
00702053	Best of Patsy Cline	$10.95
00702229	The Very Best of Creedence Clearwater Revival	$12.95
00702145	Best of Jim Croce	$10.95
00702219	David Crowder*Band Collection	$12.95
00702122	The Doors for Easy Guitar	$12.99
00702099	Best of Amy Grant	$9.95
00702190	Best of Pat Green	$19.95
00702136	Best of Merle Haggard	$10.95
00702243	Hannah Montana	$14.95
00702244	Hannah Montana 2/Meet Miley Cyrus	$16.95
00702227	Jimi Hendrix – Smash Hits	$14.99
00702236	Best of Antonio Carlos Jobim	$12.95
00702087	Best of Billy Joel	$10.95
00702245	Elton John – Greatest Hits 1970-2002	$14.99
00702204	Robert Johnson	$9.95
00702199	Norah Jones – Come Away with Me	$10.95
00702234	Selections from Toby Keith – 35 Biggest Hits	$12.95
00702003	Kiss	$9.95
00702193	Best of Jennifer Knapp	$12.95
00702097	John Lennon – Imagine	$9.95
00702216	Lynyrd Skynyrd	$14.95
00702182	The Essential Bob Marley	$12.95
00702248	Paul McCartney – All the Best	$14.99
00702129	Songs of Sarah McLachlan	$12.95
02501316	Metallica – Death Magnetic	$15.95
00702209	Steve Miller Band – Young Hearts (Greatest Hits)	$12.95
00702096	Best of Nirvana	$14.95
00702211	The Offspring – Greatest Hits	$12.95
00702030	Best of Roy Orbison	$12.95
00702144	Best of Ozzy Osbourne	$12.95
00702139	Elvis Country Favorites	$9.95
00699415	Best of Queen for Guitar	$14.99
00702208	Red Hot Chili Peppers – Greatest Hits	$12.95
00702093	Rolling Stones Collection	$17.95
00702092	Best of the Rolling Stones	$14.99
00702196	Best of Bob Seger	$12.95
00702252	Frank Sinatra – Nothing But the Best	$12.99
00702010	Best of Rod Stewart	$14.95
00702150	Best of Sting	$12.95
00702049	Best of George Strait	$12.95
00702259	Taylor Swift for Easy Guitar	$12.99
00702223	Chris Tomlin – Arriving	$12.95
00702262	Chris Tomlin Collection	$14.99
00702226	Chris Tomlin – See the Morning	$12.95
00702132	Shania Twain – Greatest Hits	$10.95
00702108	Best of Stevie Ray Vaughan	$10.95
00702123	Best of Hank Williams	$9.95
00702111	Stevie Wonder – Guitar Collection	$9.95
00702228	Neil Young – Greatest Hits	$12.99
00702188	Essential ZZ Top	$10.95

Prices, contents and availability subject to change without notice.

FOR MORE INFORMATION, SEE YOUR LOCAL MUSIC DEALER, OR WRITE TO:

HAL•LEONARD® CORPORATION
7777 W. BLUEMOUND RD. P.O. BOX 13819 MILWAUKEE, WI 53213

Visit Hal Leonard online at **www.halleonard.com**

0610

HAL•LEONARD GUITAR PLAY•ALONG®

This series will help you play your favorite songs quickly and easily. Just follow the tab and listen to the CD to hear how the guitar should sound, and then play along using the separate backing tracks. Mac or PC users can also slow down the tempo without changing pitch by using the CD in their computer. The melody and lyrics are included in the book so that you can sing or simply follow along.

INCLUDES TAB

VOL. 1 – ROCK	00699570 / $16.99
VOL. 2 – ACOUSTIC	00699569 / $16.95
VOL. 3 – HARD ROCK	00699573 / $16.95
VOL. 4 – POP/ROCK	00699571 / $16.99
VOL. 5 – MODERN ROCK	00699574 / $16.99
VOL. 6 – '90s ROCK	00699572 / $16.99
VOL. 7 – BLUES	00699575 / $16.95
VOL. 8 – ROCK	00699585 / $12.95
VOL. 9 – PUNK ROCK	00699576 / $14.95
VOL. 10 – ACOUSTIC	00699586 / $16.95
VOL. 11 – EARLY ROCK	00699579 / $14.95
VOL. 12 – POP/ROCK	00699587 / $14.95
VOL. 13 – FOLK ROCK	00699581 / $14.95
VOL. 14 – BLUES ROCK	00699582 / $16.95
VOL. 15 – R&B	00699583 / $14.95
VOL. 16 – JAZZ	00699584 / $15.95
VOL. 17 – COUNTRY	00699588 / $15.95
VOL. 18 – ACOUSTIC ROCK	00699577 / $15.95
VOL. 19 – SOUL	00699578 / $14.95
VOL. 20 – ROCKABILLY	00699580 / $14.95
VOL. 21 – YULETIDE	00699602 / $14.95
VOL. 22 – CHRISTMAS	00699600 / $15.95
VOL. 23 – SURF	00699635 / $14.95
VOL. 24 – ERIC CLAPTON	00699649 / $16.95
VOL. 25 – LENNON & McCARTNEY	00699642 / $14.95
VOL. 26 – ELVIS PRESLEY	00699643 / $14.95
VOL. 27 – DAVID LEE ROTH	00699645 / $16.95
VOL. 28 – GREG KOCH	00699646 / $14.95
VOL. 29 – BOB SEGER	00699647 / $14.95
VOL. 30 – KISS	00699644 / $16.99
VOL. 31 – CHRISTMAS HITS	00699652 / $14.95
VOL. 32 – THE OFFSPRING	00699653 / $14.95
VOL. 33 – ACOUSTIC CLASSICS	00699656 / $16.95
VOL. 34 – CLASSIC ROCK	00699658 / $16.95
VOL. 35 – HAIR METAL	00699660 / $16.95
VOL. 36 – SOUTHERN ROCK	00699661 / $16.95
VOL. 37 – ACOUSTIC METAL	00699662 / $16.95
VOL. 38 – BLUES	00699663 / $16.95
VOL. 39 – '80s METAL	00699664 / $16.99
VOL. 40 – INCUBUS	00699668 / $17.95
VOL. 41 – ERIC CLAPTON	00699669 / $16.95
VOL. 42 – CHART HITS	00699670 / $16.95
VOL. 43 – LYNYRD SKYNYRD	00699681 / $17.95
VOL. 44 – JAZZ	00699689 / $14.95
VOL. 45 – TV THEMES	00699718 / $14.95
VOL. 46 – MAINSTREAM ROCK	00699722 / $16.95
VOL. 47 – HENDRIX SMASH HITS	00699723 / $19.95
VOL. 48 – AEROSMITH CLASSICS	00699724 / $16.99
VOL. 49 – STEVIE RAY VAUGHAN	00699725 / $16.95
VOL. 50 – NÜ METAL	00699726 / $14.95
VOL. 51 – ALTERNATIVE '90s	00699727 / $12.95
VOL. 52 – FUNK	00699728 / $14.95
VOL. 53 – DISCO	00699729 / $14.99
VOL. 54 – HEAVY METAL	00699730 / $14.95
VOL. 55 – POP METAL	00699731 / $14.95
VOL. 56 – FOO FIGHTERS	00699749 / $14.95
VOL. 57 – SYSTEM OF A DOWN	00699751 / $14.95
VOL. 58 – BLINK-182	00699772 / $14.95
VOL. 59 – GODSMACK	00699773 / $14.95
VOL. 60 – 3 DOORS DOWN	00699774 / $14.95
VOL. 61 – SLIPKNOT	00699775 / $14.95
VOL. 62 – CHRISTMAS CAROLS	00699798 / $12.95
VOL. 63 – CREEDENCE CLEARWATER REVIVAL	00699802 / $16.99
VOL. 64 – THE ULTIMATE OZZY OSBOURNE	00699803 / $16.99
VOL. 65 – THE DOORS	00699806 / $16.99
VOL. 66 – THE ROLLING STONES	00699807 / $16.95
VOL. 67 – BLACK SABBATH	00699808 / $16.99
VOL. 68 – PINK FLOYD – DARK SIDE OF THE MOON	00699809 / $16.99
VOL. 69 – ACOUSTIC FAVORITES	00699810 / $14.95
VOL. 70 – OZZY OSBOURNE	00699805 / $16.99
VOL. 71 – CHRISTIAN ROCK	00699824 / $14.95
VOL. 72 – ACOUSTIC '90s	00699827 / $14.95
VOL. 73 – BLUESY ROCK	00699829 / $16.99
VOL. 74 – PAUL BALOCHE	00699831 / $14.95
VOL. 75 – TOM PETTY	00699882 / $16.99
VOL. 76 – COUNTRY HITS	00699884 / $14.95
VOL. 78 – NIRVANA	00700132 / $14.95
VOL. 80 – ACOUSTIC ANTHOLOGY	00700175 / $19.95
VOL. 81 – ROCK ANTHOLOGY	00700176 / $22.99
VOL. 82 – EASY SONGS	00700177 / $12.99
VOL. 83 – THREE CHORD SONGS	00700178 / $14.99
VOL. 84 – STEELY DAN	00700200 / $16.99
VOL. 85 – THE POLICE	00700269 / $16.99
VOL. 86 – BOSTON	00700465 / $16.99
VOL. 87 – ACOUSTIC WOMEN	00700763 / $14.99
VOL. 88 – GRUNGE	00700467 / $16.99
VOL. 91 – BLUES INSTRUMENTALS	00700505 / $14.99
VOL. 92 – EARLY ROCK INSTRUMENTALS	00700506 / $12.99
VOL. 93 – ROCK INSTRUMENTALS	00700507 / $14.99
VOL. 96 – THIRD DAY	00700560 / $14.95
VOL. 97 – ROCK BAND	00700703 / $14.99
VOL. 98 – ROCK BAND	00700704 / $14.95
VOL. 99 – ZZ TOP	00700762 / $14.99
VOL. 100 – B.B. KING	00700466 / $14.99
VOL. 102 – CLASSIC PUNK	00700769 / $14.99
VOL. 103 – SWITCHFOOT	00700773 / $16.99
VOL. 104 – DUANE ALLMAN	00700846 / $16.99
VOL. 106 – WEEZER	00700958 / $14.99
VOL. 108 – THE WHO	00701053 / $14.99
VOL. 109 – STEVE MILLER	00701054 / $14.99
VOL. 111 – JOHN MELLENCAMP	00701056 / $14.99
VOL. 113 – JIM CROCE	00701058 / $14.99
VOL. 114 – BON JOVI	00701060 / $14.99
VOL. 115 – JOHNNY CASH	00701070 / $14.99
VOL. 116 – THE VENTURES	00701124 / $14.99
VOL. 119 – AC/DC CLASSICS	00701356 / $14.99
VOL. 120 – PROGRESSIVE ROCK	00701457 / $14.99
VOL. 123 – LENNON & McCARTNEY ACOUSTIC	00701614 / $16.99

Complete song lists available online.

Prices, contents, and availability subject to change without notice.

FOR MORE INFORMATION, SEE YOUR LOCAL MUSIC DEALER, OR WRITE TO:

HAL•LEONARD® CORPORATION

7777 W. BLUEMOUND RD. P.O. BOX 13819 MILWAUKEE, WI 53213

Visit Hal Leonard online at www.halleonard.com